ONE WEEK
LOAN

This book is due for return on or before the last date shown below.

FOCUS ON SOCIAL WORK LAW
Series Editor: Alison Brammer

Palgrave Macmillan's Focus on Social Work Law series consists of compact, accessible guides to the principles, structures and processes of particular areas of the law as they apply to social work practice. Designed to develop students' understanding as well as refresh practitioners' knowledge, each book provides focused, digestible and navigable content in an easily portable form.

Available now

Looked After Children, Caroline Ball
Safeguarding Adults, Alison Brammer
Court and Legal Skills, Penny Cooper
Child Protection, Kim Holt
Capacity and Autonomy, Robert Johns
Making Good Decisions, Michael Preston-Shoot
Children in Need of Support, Joanne Westwood

Forthcoming titles

Mental Health, Christine Hutchison and Neil Hickman
Adoption and Permanency, Philip Musson
Youth Justice, Jo Staines

Author of the bestselling textbook *Social Work Law*, Alison Brammer is a qualified solicitor with specialist experience working in Social Services, including child protection, adoption, mental health and community care. Alison coordinates the MA in Child Care Law and Practice and the MA in Adult Safeguarding at Keele University.

Series Standing Order

ISBN 9781137017833 paperback
(*outside North America only*)

You can receive future titles in this series as they are published by placing a standing order. Please contact your bookseller or, in the case of difficulty, write to us at the address below with your name and address, the title of the series and the ISBN quoted above.

Customer Services Department, Macmillan Distribution Ltd
Houndmills, Basingstoke, Hampshire RG21 6XS, England

COURT AND LEGAL SKILLS

PENNY COOPER

palgrave
macmillan

First published 2014 by
PALGRAVE MACMILLAN

Palgrave Macmillan in the UK is an imprint of Macmillan Publishers Limited, registered in England, company number 785998, of Houndmills, Basingstoke, Hampshire RG21 6XS.

Palgrave Macmillan in the US is a division of St Martin's Press LLC, 175 Fifth Avenue, New York, NY 10010.

Palgrave Macmillan is the global academic imprint of the above companies and has companies and representatives throughout the world.

Palgrave® and Macmillan® are registered trademarks in the United States, the United Kingdom, Europe and other countries

ISBN: 978–1–137–36155–4

This book is printed on paper suitable for recycling and made from fully managed and sustained forest sources. Logging, pulping and manufacturing processes are expected to conform to the environmental regulations of the country of origin.

A catalogue record for this book is available from the British Library.

A catalog record for this book is available from the Library of Congress.

Typeset by Cambrian Typesetters, Camberley, Surrey

Printed in China

This book is for Michael and everyone else who struggles to make sense of the world sometimes.

CONTENTS

TABLE OF CASES

TABLE OF LEGISLATION

ACKNOWLEDGMENTS

There are many people who have been a source of inspiration in my work and helped with this book. I would like to acknowledge them for their professional efforts in their respective fields and for their support of mine. In particular I am grateful to Amy Croft, Gill Darvill, Chantelle Delacroix, Helen Caunce, Joanne Haswell, Angela Henriques, Fleur Heyworth, Reg Hooke, Dorothy Kwagala-Igaga, Mick King, Jane Lyndsay, Ruth Marchant, Beth Phillips, Sharon Richardson, Sue Thurman, Bridget Towning, Brendan O'Mahony, Kevin Smith, Susan Watson, Jaqueline Wheatcroft, David Wurtzel and Rosemary Wyatt. Thanks above all go to my heroes, Bob, Chris and Bobby.

The author and publisher would like to thank the NSPCC for its permission to reproduce extracts from J Plotnikoff and R Woolfson (2009) *Measuring Up? Evaluating Implementation of Government Commitments to Young Witnesses in Criminal Proceedings* (London: NSPCC/Nuffield Foundation).

This book contains public sector information licensed under the Open Government Licence v2.0.

ABBREVIATIONS

ABE	Achieving Best Evidence (MoJ, 2011)
ADR	Alternative Dispute Resolution
ATC	Advocacy Training Council
Cafcass	Children and Family Court Advisory and Support Service
CICA	Criminal Injuries Compensation Authority
CPS	Crown Prosecution Service
CV	curriculum vitae
DCMS	Department of Culture, Media and Sport
DCSF	Department for Children, Schools and Families
DPP	Director of Public Prosecutions, the head of the CPS
ECHR	European Convention on Human Rights
EWHC	High Court of Justice of England and Wales (the abbreviation is used in neutral citations on judgments)
EWCA	Court of Appeal of England and Wales (the abbreviation is used in neutral citations on judgments)
FDAC	Family Drug and Alcohol Court
IDVA	independent domestic violence adviser
IMCA	independent mental capacity advocate
ISO	independent social worker
ISVA	independent sexual violence adviser
LCJ	Lord Chief Justice
LIP	litigant in person
MoJ	Ministry of Justice
NSPCC	National Society for the Prevention of Cruelty to Children
OPG	Office of the Public Guardian
PACE	Police and Criminal Evidence Act 1984
PLO	Public Law Outline Practice Direction 12A – a system for judicial case management in Children Act 1989 public law cases
QC	Queen's Counsel
RI	registered intermediary

R v   'R' is the abbreviated form of *regina* meaning 'The Queen' and 'v' stands for versus, or against, because it is the state which prosecutes. The name of the case therefore indicates that it is the Queen against the name of the person, or organization, being prosecuted.

SENDIST   Special Educational Needs and Disability Tribunal

SIDS   sudden infant death syndrome

UKSC   United Kingdom Supreme Court (the abbreviation is used in neutral citations on judgments)

VPS   victim personal statement

WIS   Witness Intermediary Scheme

USING THIS BOOK

Aim of the series

Welcome to the Focus on Social Work Law Series.

This introductory section aims to elucidate the aims and philosophy of the series; introduce some key themes that run through the series; outline the key features within each volume; and offer a brief legal skills guide to complement use of the series.

The Social Work Law Focus Series provides a distinct range of specialist resources for students and practitioners. Each volume provides an accessible and practical discussion of the law applicable to a particular area of practice. The length of each volume ensures that whilst portable and focused there is nevertheless a depth of coverage of each topic beyond that typically contained in comprehensive textbooks addressing all aspects of social work law and practice.

Each volume includes the relevant principles, structures and processes of the law (with case law integrated into the text) and highlights clearly the application of the law to practice. A key objective for each text is to identify the policy context of each area of practice and the factors that have shaped the law into its current presentation. As law is constantly developing and evolving, where known, likely future reform of the law is identified. Each book takes a critical approach, noting inconsistencies, omissions and other challenges faced by those charged with its implementation.

The significance of the Human Rights Act 1998 to social work practice is a common theme in each text and implications of the Act for practice in the particular area are identified with inclusion of relevant case law.

The series focuses on the law in England and Wales. Some references may be made to comparable aspects of law in Scotland and Northern Ireland, particularly to highlight differences in approach. With devolution in Scotland and the expanding role of the Welsh Assembly Government it will be important for practitioners in those areas and working at the borders to be familiar with any such differences.

Features

At a glance content lists

Each chapter begins with a bullet point list summarizing the key points within the topic included in that chapter. From this list the reader can see 'at a glance' how the materials are organized and what to expect in that section. The introductory chapter provides an overview of the book, outlining coverage in each chapter that enables the reader to see how the topic develops throughout the text. The boundaries of the discussion are set including, where relevant, explicit recognition of areas that are excluded from the text.

Key case analysis

One of the key aims of the series is to emphasize an integrated understanding of law, comprising legislation and case law and practice. For this reason each chapter includes at least one key case analysis feature focusing on a particularly significant case. The facts of the case are outlined in brief followed by analysis of the implications of the decision for social work practice in a short commentary. Given the significance of the selected cases, readers are encouraged to follow up references and read the case in full together with any published commentaries.

On-the-spot questions

These questions are designed to consolidate learning and prompt reflection on the material considered. These questions may be used as a basis for discussion with colleagues or fellow students and may also prompt consideration or further investigation of how the law is applied within a particular setting or authority, for example, looking at information provided to service users on a council website. Questions may also follow key cases, discussion of research findings or practice scenarios, focusing on the issues raised and application of the relevant law to practice.

Practice focus

Each volume incorporates practice-focused case scenarios to demonstrate how the law is applied to social work practice. The scenarios may be fictional or based on an actual decision.

Further reading

Each chapter closes with suggestions for further reading to develop knowledge and critical understanding. Annotated to explain the reasons for inclusion, the reader may be directed to classic influential pieces, such as enquiry reports, up-to-date research and analysis of issues discussed in the chapter, and relevant policy documents. In addition students may wish to read in full the case law included throughout the text and to follow up references integrated into discussion of each topic.

Websites

As further important sources of information, websites are also included in the text with links from the companion website. Some may be a gateway to access significant documents including government publications, others may provide accessible information for service users or present a particular perspective on an area, such as the voices of experts by experience. Given the rapid development of law and practice across the range of topics covered in the series, reference to relevant websites can be a useful way to keep pace with actual and anticipated changes.

Glossary

Each text includes a subject-specific glossary of key terms for quick reference and clarification. A flashcard version of the glossary is available on the companion website.

Visual aids

As appropriate, visual aids are included where information may be presented accessibly as a table, graph or flow chart. This approach is particularly helpful for the presentation of some complex areas of law and to demonstrate structured decision-making or options available.

Companion site

The series-wide companion site www.palgrave.com/socialworklaw provides additional learning resources, including flashcard glossaries, web links, a legal skills guide, and a blog to communicate important developments and updates. The site will also host a student feedback zone.

Key sources of law

In this section an outline of the key sources of law considered throughout the series is provided. The following 'Legal skills' section includes some guidance on the easiest ways to access and understand these sources.

Legislation

The term legislation is used interchangeably with Acts of Parliament and statutes to refer to primary sources of law.

All primary legislation is produced through the parliamentary process, beginning its passage as a Bill. Bills may have their origins as an expressed policy in a government manifesto, in the work of the Law Commission, or following and responding to a significant event such as a child death or the work of a government department such as the Home Office.

Each Bill is considered by both the House of Lords and House of Commons, debated and scrutinized through various committee stages before becoming an Act on receipt of royal assent.

Legislation has a title and year, for example, the Equality Act 2010. Legislation can vary in length from an Act with just one section to others with over a hundred. Lengthy Acts are usually divided into headed 'Parts' (like chapters) containing sections, subsections and paragraphs. For example, s. 31 of the Children Act 1989 is in Part IV entitled 'Care and Supervision' and outlines the criteria for care order applications. Beyond the main body of the Act the legislation may also include 'Schedules' following the main provisions. Schedules have the same force of law as the rest of the Act but are typically used to cover detail such as a list of legislation which has been amended or revoked by the current Act or detailed matters linked to a specific provision, for instance, Schedule 2 of the Children Act 1989 details specific services (e.g. day centres) which may be provided under the duty to safeguard and promote the welfare of children in need, contained in s. 17.

Remember also that statutes often contain sections dealing with interpretation or definitions and, although often situated towards the end of the Act, these can be a useful starting point.

Legislation also includes Statutory Instruments which may be in the form of rules, regulations and orders. The term delegated legislation collectively describes this body of law as it is made under delegated authority of Parliament, usually by a minister or government department. Statutory Instruments tend to provide additional detail to the outline scheme provided by the primary legislation, the Act of Parliament. Statutory Instruments are usually cited by year and a number, for example, Local Authority Social Services (Complaints Procedure) Order SI 2006/1681.

Various documents may be issued to further assist with the implementation of legislation including guidance and codes of practice.

Guidance

Guidance documents may be described as formal or practice guidance. Formal guidance may be identified as such where it is stated to have been issued under s. 7(1) of the Local Authority Social Services Act 1970, which provides that 'local authorities shall act under the general guidance of the Secretary of State'. An example of s. 7 guidance is *Working Together to Safeguard Children* (2013, London: Department of Health). The significance of s. 7 guidance was explained by Sedley J in *R v London Borough of Islington, ex parte Rixon* [1997] ELR 66: 'Parliament in enacting s. 7(1) did not intend local authorities to whom ministerial guidance was given to be free, having considered it, to take it or leave it . . . in my view parliament by s. 7(1) has required local authorities to follow the path charted by the Secretary of State's guidance, with liberty to deviate from it where the local authority judges on admissible grounds that there is good reason to do so, but without freedom to take a substantially different course.' (71)

Practice guidance does not carry s. 7 status but should nevertheless normally be followed as setting examples of what good practice might look like.

Codes of practice

Codes of practice have been issued to support the Mental Health Act 1983 and the Mental Capacity Act 2005. Again, it is a matter of good practice to follow the recommendations of the codes and these lengthy documents include detailed and illustrative scenarios to assist with interpretation and application of the legislation. There may also be a duty on specific people charged with responsibilities under the primary legislation to have regard to the code.

Guidance and codes of practice are available on relevant websites, for example, the Department of Health, as referenced in individual volumes.

Case law

Case law provides a further major source of law. In determining disputes in court the judiciary applies legislation. Where provisions within legislation are unclear or ambiguous the judiciary follows principles of statutory interpretation but at times judges are quite creative.

Some areas of law are exclusively contained in case law and described as common law. Most law of relevance to social work practice is of relatively recent origin and has its primary basis in legislation. Case law remains relevant as it links directly to such legislation and may clarify and explain provisions and terminology within the legislation. The significance of a particular decision will depend on the position of the court in a hierarchy whereby the Supreme Court is most senior and the Magistrates' Court is junior. Decisions of the higher courts bind the lower courts – they must be followed. This principle is known as the doctrine of precedent. Much legal debate takes place as to the precise element of a ruling which subsequently binds other decisions. This is especially the case where in the Court of Appeal or Supreme Court there are between three and five judges hearing a case, majority judgments are allowed and different judges may arrive at the same conclusion but for different reasons. Where a judge does not agree with the majority, the term dissenting judgment is applied.

It is important to understand how cases reach court. Many cases in social work law are based on challenges to the way a local authority has exercised its powers. This is an aspect of administrative law known as judicial review where the central issue for the court is not the substance of the decision taken by the authority but the way it was taken. Important considerations will be whether the authority has exceeded its powers, failed to follow established procedures or acted irrationally.

Before an individual can challenge an authority in judicial review it will usually be necessary to exhaust other remedies first, including local authority complaints procedures. If unsatisfied with the outcome of a complaint an individual has a further option which is to complain to the Local Government Ombudsman (LGO). The LGO investigates alleged cases of maladministration and may make recommendations to local authorities including the payment of financial compensation. Ombudsman decisions may be accessed on the LGO website and make interesting reading. In cases involving social services, a common concern across children's and adults' services is unreasonable delay in carrying out assessments and providing services. See www.lgo.org.uk.

Classification of law

The above discussion related to the sources and status of laws. It is also important to note that law can serve a variety of functions and may be grouped into recognized classifications. For law relating to social work practice key classifications distinguish between law which is criminal or civil and law which is public or private.

Whilst acknowledging the importance of these classifications, it must also be appreciated that individual concerns and circumstances may not always fall so neatly into the same categories, a given scenario may engage with criminal, civil, public and private law.

- Criminal law relates to alleged behaviour which is defined by statute or common law as an offence prosecuted by the state, carrying a penalty which may include imprisonment. The offence must be proved 'beyond reasonable doubt'.
- Civil law is the term applied to all other areas of law and often focuses on disputes between individuals. A lower standard of proof, 'balance of probabilities', applies in civil cases.
- Public law is that in which society has some interest and involves a public authority, such as care proceedings.
- Private law operates between individuals, such as marriage or contract.

Legal skills guide: accessing and understanding the law

Legislation

Legislation may be accessed as printed copies published by The Stationery Office and is also available online. Some books on a particular area of law will include a copy of the Act (sometimes annotated) and this is a useful way of learning about new laws. As time goes by, however, and amendments are made to legislation it can become increasingly difficult to keep track of the up-to-date version of an Act. Revised and up-to-date versions of legislation (as well as the version originally enacted) are available on the website www.legislation.gov.uk.

Legislation may also be accessed on the Parliament website. Here, it is possible to trace the progress of current and draft Bills and a link to Hansard provides transcripts of debates on Bills as they pass through both Houses of Parliament, www.parliament.uk.

Bills and new legislation are often accompanied by 'Explanatory notes' which can give some background to the development of the new law and offer useful explanations of each provision.

Case law

Important cases are reported in law reports available in traditional bound volumes (according to court, specialist area or general weekly reports) or online. Case referencing is known as citation and follows particular conventions according to whether a hard copy law report or online version is sought.

Citation of cases in law reports begins with the names of the parties, followed by the year and volume number of the law report, followed by an abbreviation of the law report title, then the page number. For example: *Lawrence v Pembrokeshire CC* [2007] 2 FLR 705. The case is reported in volume 2 of the 2007 Family Law Report at page 705.

Online citation, sometimes referred to as neutral citation because it is not linked to a particular law report, also starts with the names of the parties, followed by the year in which the case was decided, followed by an abbreviation of the court in which the case was heard, followed by a number representing the place in the order of cases decided by that court. For example: *R (Macdonald) v Royal Borough of Kensington and Chelsea* [2011] UKSC 33. Neutral citation of this case shows that it was a 2011 decision of the Supreme Court.

University libraries tend to have subscriptions to particular legal databases, such as 'Westlaw', which can be accessed by those enrolled as students, often via direct links from the university library webpage. Westlaw and LexisNexis are especially useful as sources of case law, statutes and other legal materials. Libraries usually have their own guides to these sources, again often published on their websites. For most cases there is a short summary or analysis as well as the full transcript.

As not everyone using the series will be enrolled at a university, the following website can be accessed without any subscription: BAILII (British and Irish Legal Information Institute) www.bailii.org. This site includes judgments from the full range of UK court services including the Supreme Court, Court of Appeal and High Court but also features a wide range of tribunal decisions. Judgments for Scotland, Northern Ireland and the Republic of Ireland are also available as are judgments of the European Court of Human Rights.

Whether accessed via a law report or online, the presentation of cases follows a template. The report begins with the names of the parties, the court which heard the cases, names(s) of the judges(s) and dates of the hearing. This is followed by a summary of key legal issues involved in the case (often in italics) known as catchwords, then the headnote, which is a paragraph or so stating the key facts of the case and the nature of the claim or dispute or the criminal charge. 'HELD' indicates the ruling of the court. This is followed by a list of cases that were referred to in legal argument during the hearing, a summary of the journey of the case through appeal processes, names of the advocates and then the start of the full judgment(s) given by the judge(s). The judgment usually recounts the circumstances of the case, findings of fact and findings on the law and reasons for the decision.

If stuck on citations the Cardiff Index to Legal Abbreviations is a useful resource at www.legalabbrevs.cardiff.ac.uk.

There are numerous specific guides to legal research providing more detailed examination of legal materials but the best advice on developing legal skills is to start exploring the above and to read some case law – it's surprisingly addictive!

1

SOCIAL WORKERS IN THE ENGLISH LEGAL SYSTEM

From day one in practice a social worker is required to work within the law, for example, to handle case files and information in accordance with the Data Protection Act 1998 and the Human Rights Act 1998. In practice it is not always obvious that departmental guidance and local authority policies are actually reflecting law and legal requirements. As a trainee social worker you will have learnt about aspects of law as part of your training. This book builds on that knowledge and tackles the practical detail of how to get things done in a way that will make dealing with **lawyers** and courts a more effective and rewarding experience for you and your service users. (I have used the term 'service user' throughout this book though I recognize that sometimes social workers will use other terms such as 'client' or 'customer'.)

Most social workers will come into contact with the legal system as part of their professional practice; it is part and parcel of being a social worker. Once involved in a legal matter you play a key part in ensuring the court reaches a just result. It is not hard to think of examples of cases where social work **evidence** could be crucial to the outcome at court – a parent and child facing permanent separation, an elderly person requiring specialist residential care, a **defendant** facing conviction or a patient needing lifesaving treatment. The aim of this book is to ensure that social workers have the necessary knowledge and skills to understand procedure for court and present the evidence to the highest possible standard. We know that training is essential and can have a direct bearing on the case results.

> [T]training social workers in the procedural and presentational aspects of courts improves their ability to produce a care case that is more likely to achieve best outcomes for the child or young person. (Munro, 2011:101)

It is envisaged that this book will be a training and a practice companion that will be read chapter by chapter and later dipped into as a quick reference guide as and when required.

This book begins with the law and best practice on record-keeping and information-sharing so that your files will pass muster at court and will be the basis of excellent evidence. Subsequent chapters cover statements for court, presenting your evidence effectively in court (even under **cross-examination**), supporting vulnerable service users in the legal system and getting the most out of working relationships with other professionals, such as police officers, **intermediaries** and expert

witnesses. The final chapter is about dealing with the aftermath of hearings and future legal reforms.

Daunting as the legal system might be, it is also a tool for social workers to achieve better outcomes for their service users, for instance, by obtaining a court order to remove an abused child from harm, seeking an order to secure a residential placement for a mentally incapacitated service user, or going to court to give support for a vulnerable defendant in a criminal trial. Or it could be that the social worker has been required to respond to legal proceedings, for instance, providing a statement to the police as a witness to an assault, giving evidence at a public enquiry about the death of a child, responding to a request by the Crown Prosecution Service (CPS) for the disclosure of confidential service user records or supporting a vulnerable victim in a prosecution.

Invariably, being involved in a legal matter creates stress. Sometimes the media become involved and this ratchets up the pressure even more. Social work can create some of the most striking newspaper headlines. Serious case reviews, such as those in relation to the boys known as the 'Edlington two' (Carlile, 2012), the death of 'Baby P' (Haringey Local Safeguarding Children Board, 2009) and the death of Daniel Pelka (Coventry Local Safeguarding Children Board, 2013), are also reminders of the challenges facing social workers.

The *Daily Telegraph* on 30 November 2013 ran a story: 'Child taken from womb then put into care. Exclusive: Essex social services have obtained a court order against a woman that allowed her to be forcibly sedated and for her child to be taken from her womb by caesarean section' (Freeman, 2013). It related to ongoing legal proceedings and Essex County Council's response on 2 December 2013 (an extract of which is below) provided a much needed counterbalance to the newspaper reports:

> The Health Trust had been looking after the mother since 13 June 2012 under section 3 of the Mental Health Act [1983]. Because of their concerns the Health Trust contacted Essex County Council's Social Services. Five weeks later it was the Health Trust's clinical decision to apply to the High Court for permission to deliver her unborn baby by caesarean section because of concerns about risks to mother and child. The mother was able to see her baby on the day of birth and the following day. Essex County Council's Social Services obtained an Interim Care Order from the County Court because the mother was too unwell to

> care for her child. Historically, the mother has two other children which she is unable to care for due to orders made by the Italian authorities. In accordance with Essex County Council's Social Services practice social workers liaised extensively with the extended family before and after the birth of the baby, to establish if anyone could care for the child.
>
> *Essex County Council, 2013*

The issues in this case show just how challenging and difficult casework decisions can be. Less than a month before those headlines about the Essex case, in the same national newspaper, Childline founder Esther Rantzen wrote 'if we create an atmosphere of unforgiving rage around all social workers, we will never attract people of real talent'. ('Sharon Shoesmith: villain? Victim? Or someone who got it wrong?', Rantzen, 2013). Fortunately, judges do not permit 'an atmosphere of unforgiving rage' around social workers or anyone else in their courts. Judges have a duty to ensure that hearings are fair and in order for that to happen the evidence must be presented and considered in a calm and objective way.

Judges appreciate that most social workers are short on time and resources. The role carried out by social workers is constantly under scrutiny.

> Social workers are among the most essential yet maligned of public servants. They are criticized to such an extent that their work is often discussed and their profession roundly disparaged by the public at large. In contrast, little, if anything, is ever heard of their successes. The reality, however, of social work in the United Kingdom, is far from the commonly held public perception.
>
> *All Party Parliamentary Group on Social Work, 2013:5*

Cases where things have gone wrong are invariably the ones that hit the newspaper headlines despite the fact that they are not the norm of day-to-day practice; social work successes or failed actions against social workers do not tend to sell newspapers. This book in part will redress that as it aims to present key cases in a balanced way. Reading and reflecting on key cases, practice-focused examples and doing 'on-the-spot' questions will help demystify the legal system, reduce wasted time and make legal tasks more straightforward. As has been said many times about the law, it is a framework not a barrier, and this book's goal is to illustrate how useful that framework can be.

Social workers in the English legal system

The English legal system covers England and Wales (Scotland and Northern Ireland have their own legal systems; even Welsh law differs in some respects where the Welsh government has passed its own laws which differ from those in England). The supreme law of the land is an Act of Parliament, also called primary legislation. There is no single document which can be called 'the constitution' but the phrase is sometimes used to indicate the totality of laws, the various organs of government, the courts and the civil service. The 'common law' is made up of judicial decisions which have grown up over time, and which create 'judicial precedents'. That is, if the Court of Appeal says 'in these circumstances, the law is X' then every judge in a lower court must interpret the law accordingly. One way to think of the difference between legislation and common law (judge-made law) is that common law fills the gaps left by legislation, i.e., where there is no legislation or how to interpret existing legislation is not clear, we look to case law for clarification of the law.

When courts interpret an Act of Parliament they must interpret it as far as possible so as to make it compatible (consistent) with the Human Rights Act 1998. A High Court judge, the Court of Appeal and/or the Supreme Court can declare an Act (or part of an Act) to be 'incompatible' with the Human Rights Act 1998 but it is then left to ministers to decide whether, when and how to amend the legislation.

Europe and the European Convention on Human Rights

Parliament is obliged to incorporate into English law European Union directives. Examples are data protection and anti-discrimination on grounds of age. In addition, the European Convention on Human Rights (ECHR) sets out fundamental rights and freedoms. For example, Article 3 prohibits torture and 'inhuman or degrading treatment or punishment'. Article 6 states that 'everyone is entitled to a fair and public hearing within a reasonable time by an independent and impartial tribunal established by law'. Article 8 provides the right to respect for private and family life. The British government signed up to the ECHR in 1950; it was incorporated into domestic law by the Human Rights Act 1998. From time to time, British citizens have taken their cases to the European Court of Human Rights in Strasbourg (distinct from the European Court in Luxembourg). On almost every occasion when the court has ruled against the British government, the government has altered the law unless it has been altered already.

An example of how legislation can arise

The Victoria Climbié Inquiry report with its 108 recommendations for reform marked a watershed in social work (Laming, 2003). In June 2003 the House of Commons Health Committee quoted and endorsed the words of Peter Beresford, a professor of social policy at Brunel University:

> Her death has become one of those major modern occasions where there seems to have been a collective sense of empathy for a stranger's fate. She has become an embodiment of the betrayal, vulnerability and public abandonment of children.
>
> The inquiry must mark the end of child protection policy built on a hopeless process of child care tragedy, scandal, inquiry, findings, brief media interest and ad hoc political response. There is now a rare chance to take stock and rebuild.
>
> *House of Commons Select Committee, 2003:3*

The government did indeed take stock and part of that process involved issuing a consultation paper (known as a government Green Paper) called *Every Child Matters*. The foreword by the then Prime Minister, Tony Blair, contained these words: 'Responding to the inquiry headed by Lord Laming into Victoria's death, we are proposing here a range of measures to reform and improve children's care.' (HM Government, 2003:1) After the consultation there were proposals put forward for new laws which resulted in legislation including the Children Act 2004 that included a requirement for Local Safeguarding Children Boards and much better cooperation between agencies to safeguard and promote the welfare of children.

Within the English legal system there are judges sitting in various courts and tribunals applying the law to the disputes that come before them. Tribunals are less formal decision-making bodies but follow similar procedures to courts. Taking a matter to court requires resources. A case begins when one side (or 'party') starts legal proceedings against another. For example, a local authority starts care proceedings or the CPS authorizes a defendant to be charged with a crime. Parties are either funded from the public purse, including through legal aid, or, if they have their own resources, they may fund their own legal representation.

Some people represent themselves in proceedings (litigants in person (LIPs)) and some are represented by lawyers. 'Lawyer' is an umbrella term that includes solicitors, barristers, legal executives and paralegals. (Professionals that social workers regularly encounter in the legal system are discussed in detail in Chapter 5.)

The English legal system can be thought of in three parts: criminal, civil and family justice. What follows is a brief overview. There are many books on the English legal system, two of which are listed at the end of this chapter.

In criminal law, the state (acting as 'the Crown') brings charges against an individual because he or she is suspected of having committed an offence. A case is usually referred to by name starting *R v*, for example, *R v Joseph Bloggs*. *R* is short for Regina i.e. the Queen who is the head of state, as it is the state that prosecutes.

The state also maintains the police, the courts, the CPS and provides most of the funding for defence solicitors and barristers. Because of the position of the state (i.e. resources and relative power), certain rights are embedded in the system, such as the accused's right to silence. The state has the responsibility of proving that the offence has been committed. The court's role is to determine criminal responsibility and, if found guilty, to sentence the offender.

How a social worker might be involved:

- A social worker based in a hospital witnesses a patient assault a member of the healthcare staff and is asked to provide a statement to the police.
- A local authority foster child has been assaulted by a worker in a care home. The care worker claims to have been acting in self-defence. The social worker is contacted by the solicitor representing the care worker and asked to be a defence witness at the Crown Court trial.
- A teenage girl who has had contact with children's services in the past has disclosed to the police that she has been sexually abused by her

uncle. The uncle's defence lawyers seek disclosure of social work records in relation to the girl. The social worker is asked to identify and supply the records.

Civil cases only come before the courts because one party has sued another. The state acts as an umpire in these disputes, by providing a court system to decide the issues expeditiously and proportionately and to enforce the judge's eventual decision. Where there is a wrong, the court seeks to find a remedy.

Tribunals form part of the civil justice system and they cover a wide range of matters, for example, employment, immigration and asylum, mental health, school exclusions and special educational needs (in the Special Educational Needs and Disability Tribunal (SENDIST)).

How a social worker might be involved:

- A foster carer is suing the local authority in the civil court for damages alleging that she was not told about the dangers posed by the foster child who was placed with her; the social worker who placed the child with her is required to provide a statement about what she knew and what she told the foster parent.
- A former colleague of the social worker has left his job in the local authority and is claiming unfair dismissal. His solicitor writes to the social worker and asks her to provide a statement for the case he is bringing against her former employer in the employment tribunal.

The Court of Protection has the same authority as the High Court. It has jurisdiction over the property, financial affairs and personal welfare of those who lack the mental capacity to take decisions themselves. In *A v Independent News & Media Ltd and Others* [2010], the Lord Chief Justice of England and Wales said:

> [t]he Court of Protection was created by the Mental Capacity Act 2005. The Court has been vested with significant powers to assist those who, for whatever reason, lack the capacity to make decisions themselves. [17]

The court can appoint deputies to act on behalf of people who are unable to make decisions about their personal health, finance or welfare. Up until 2010 there was no single place to find the **judgments** of the Court of Protection but they are now reported on the website of the British and Irish Legal Information Institute (BAILII) and some key cases also appear on the website of the Office of the Public Guardian (OPG). By way of example, the Court of Protection might hear a case when:

- The local authority is in dispute with the parents of a 40-year-old man with autism about where he should live. The social worker is asked to supply a witness statement in support of the local authority's application to the Court of Protection for a declaration about where the vulnerable adult should live.
- The local authority is applying to govern the personal affairs of a learning disabled woman with cerebral palsy and global developmental delay. The social worker is called to give evidence about her service user's mental capacity.
- It is unclear if it would be lawful to prevent sexual relations between a brain-injured woman and her partner (this was the issue in *IM v LM and Another* [2014]) and the social worker is asked to give her opinion on what is in the woman's best interests.

Family law is also about disputes between parties. They are usually, as the name suggests, members of the same family. The state has a pro-active role in ensuring the welfare of children. 'Public' law cases involve the local authority seeking an order in relation to a child/children and 'private law' cases are those where the parties in dispute are usually the individuals (such as parents in dispute about where their child should live). The purpose of proceedings in relation to children, whether private or public, is to determine the best outcome for the child. The court's role is not to determine criminal responsibility or punishment.

How a social worker might be involved:

- Parents are in dispute with each other about whom their children should live with and they have made cross-allegations of neglect. The judge in the private family law proceedings has asked for a report by a local authority social worker detailing the children's circumstances.
- The local authority is planning to issue applications for care orders in respect of three children who it is believed are likely to suffer significant harm if they remain in the care of the parents. The social worker to the children is required to provide written evidence, including a statement to accompany the application.

Avoiding court and alternative dispute resolution in civil and family cases

Over the last 15 years in civil and private law family matters there has been an increasing emphasis on avoiding going to court. There is an expectation that, even before issuing court proceedings, attempts should be made to negotiate a settlement and avoid legal proceedings. This expectation includes the party who is seeking the remedy sending a 'letter before action' (also called 'a letter before proceedings') setting out what the other side should do to avoid the matter going to court. In civil cases it is very usual for a mediator (a neutral third party) to assist with negoti- ations. Legal aid (public funding) is scarcely available for anyone wishing to litigate a civil or private family dispute. Government policy is to steer parties towards alternative dispute resolution (ADR), namely mediation.

The Family Drug and Alcohol Court (FDAC) has established a new style of court proceedings. It began as a pilot at the Inner London Family Proceedings Court and is also being piloted in other parts of the coun- try. The court hearings are more collaborative, more frequent, closely managed by the same judge each time and at some court review meet- ings lawyers do not attend at all. A multidisciplinary team works closely with the parents and the court. Parents volunteer for the FDAC project and can opt out, in which case care proceedings will continue in the standard way in the Family Court. In future, where the main issue affect- ing parenting is drug and/or alcohol misuse, FDAC may become more common as an ADR method.

Family justice reform

Following a major review of family justice for the government, carried out by David Norgrove (*Family Justice Review Final Report*, November 2011), the government aims to implement a number of reforms by way of new legislation. Some of these are set out below.

The Children and Families Act 2014 includes provisions to:

- make it a requirement to attend a family mediation information and assessment meeting before applying for certain private law orders;
- ensure courts take account of the principle that both parents should continue to be involved in their children's lives where that

is safe and consistent with the child's welfare, which remains the court's paramount consideration;

- replace the terms 'residence' and 'contact orders' with 'child arrangements orders';
- ensure that expert evidence in family proceedings concerning children is permitted only when 'necessary';
- introduce a maximum 26-week time limit for completing care and supervision proceedings with the possibility of extending the time limit in a particular case for up to eight weeks at a time should that be necessary to resolve the proceedings justly.

One of the most noteworthy proposals is that proceedings for care/supervision orders under the Children Act 1989 should be completed within 26 weeks. For some 20 years or so, applications for care orders have typically taken about a year from start to finish. Repeated efforts over the years to reduce this have failed. It remains to be seen if the legislation will have the desired effect. In any event the time pressures and expectations on social workers have dramatically increased in this area as a result of requirements for better quality local authority applications. This is discussed in detail in Chapter 3.

Coroner's Court

The Coroner's Court is unique in that it is a forum for examining the circumstances surrounding a death which was: violent or unnatural; occurred when a person was in state detention, including prison/police custody; occurred when a person was detained under the Mental Health Act 1983; or when the cause of death is still uncertain after a post-mortem. The coroner conducts, with or without a jury, a fact-finding inquiry to establish reliable answers to the following questions:

- Who was the deceased?
- When and where did the deceased die?
- How and in what circumstances did the deceased die?

This is a fact-finding exercise – it is not **adversarial**, and there are no formal allegations or claims for a remedy.

How a social worker might be involved:

- A teenage boy who is the subject of a care order made in the Family Courts is arrested and dies whilst in custody. An inquest is held and the child's social worker is called to give evidence.

- A learning disabled adult in semi-independent living disappears from her accommodation and is later found dead. She died a violent death and the social worker is asked to give evidence at the inquest.

Overlap

There can be an overlap between the areas. For example, if there is an allegation that a mother with a mental disorder is endangering her health and that of her unborn child, an application may be made to the Court of Protection to intervene to safeguard the mother, and care proceedings may be required in the Family Courts in respect of the child. The mother might later sue for damages in the civil courts on the basis that the local authority took action contrary to her human rights. If a criminal offence is suspected, the police will investigate and the CPS may decide to prosecute, which of course would take place in the criminal courts.

PRACTICE FOCUS

Imagine you are Amina's social worker. She is 22. A psychology report states that she has an IQ of 49 and has limited intellectual capacity. She has a history of challenging behaviour and underage sexual relations. She also has a history of disrupted placements and currently lives in supported lodgings. Six months ago she began a relationship with a 30-year-old man she calls 'Sunny'. Amina tells you she has been raped by Sunny and is now pregnant. She says he takes her money and doesn't like her speaking to you. Amina says she wants to get away from Sunny but she doesn't know how.

- What would you do to help Amina?
- How does the law assist you to help Amina?

Who are the judges?

One of the main reasons why our legal system is held in such high regard around the world is because our judges are independent. They are not elected nor are they appointed by the government. That is not to say that our judicial system is perfect or without its critics. Of concern to many is that, at least at a senior level, the judiciary is predominantly white and male. Calls have been made for positive action at the appointments stage so that the judiciary might better reflect the ethnic and gender make-up of society as a whole.

Academics have conducted research into the working lives of judges. In her 2011 book *Sitting in Judgment: The Working Lives of Judges*, Professor Penny Darbyshire interviewed and shadowed 77 judges in Crown Courts, plus some 'bonus' judges including senior ones. Through direct observation she found that the old stereotypes do not hold and debunked a myth about most judges being out of touch, old, pompous etc. Many of the judges in this study opened up to her in extraordinarily frank ways and in so doing come across as very human and grounded in the real world (Darbyshire, 2011).

In their 2013 book *Family Justice: The Work of Family Judges in Uncertain Times*, John Eekelaar and Mavis Maclean studied 12 judges in ten different courts between February 2009 and August 2010. One observation revealed:

> a day listed as the first day of a five-day final care hearing turned out to be a complex interweaving of three hearings: an adoption case requiring a witness summons, care plans being reappraised in a case management hearing, and forensic questioning of a witness in the case originally listed for that day. The day was characterized by the judge's need to be flexible, relisting matters as circumstances changed, and maintaining familiarity with the detail of a number of cases at once.
>
> *Eekelaar and Maclean, 2013:109*

The study highlighted the interventionist nature of the judge's role in a family case which can be contrasted with the role of judges in criminal cases where the purpose and the issues are very different.

> In each case, both public law and private law [family] matters, these Circuit Court judges clearly did not simply choose between two legal arguments put forward in an adversarial way about what should happen to a particular child, but went beyond this to scrutinize and modify the work of the professionals involved, actively promoting the best possible outcome for the child.
>
> *Eekelaar and Maclean, 2013:111*

The authors noted that 'from what we observed, judges (and the Legal Adviser) were unfailingly courteous and helpful to all parties, as also were the court staff'.

There is a hierarchy to the judges and the courts. The most senior court in this country is the Supreme Court (where we still only have and have only ever had one female Supreme Court Justice). Below the Supreme Court is the Court of Appeal. Courts where trials or final hearings are heard sit below the appeal courts. These are all the other courts and tribunals including the High Court, County Court, Family Courts, Crown Courts and Magistrates' Courts and tribunals.

If you are going to court you might be wondering what to call the judge in court. Your lawyer or the usher is usually able to tell you and it is worth asking because it can be confusing as there are often exceptions to the rule. For example, in a jury trial the judge would normally be 'Your Honour' but in the Old Bailey (the Central Criminal Court) the judges are 'My Lord' or 'My Lady'. Some of the most useful examples are set out below.

Courts/tribunals you might appear in as a social worker	What to call the judge
Family Courts	Sir or Madam (unless it is the High Court in which case it is My Lord/My Lady)
Court of Protection	My Lord or My Lady (as it is in the High Court)
Magistrates' Court	Sir or Madam (some still use 'Your Worship' though that tends to be used less these days)
Crown Court	Your Honour (usually but there are some exceptions)
Tribunals (e.g. the Immigration, Employment, Special Educational Needs and Disability Tribunals)	Sir or Madam

Table 1.1: Addressing the judge

The website of the judiciary (www.judiciary.gov.uk) has a section entitled 'What do I call a judge?' It details how to address judges in court and how to address them when writing to them. This is more likely to be of use to your lawyers than to you, the social worker. In court as a witness it is not usually necessary to preface what you say with anything; you can simply answer the question. If you do want to address the judge in court and do not know or cannot remember how to address them, you can simply use 'Sir' or 'Madam' as the case may be. That is unlikely to cause any offence, whoever the judge is. If you meet a judge outside court, for example, at a conference or at a training event, calling them 'Judge' is accepted practice as in 'Pleased to meet you, Judge'.

Judges should always be addressed with respect whatever their level and even if you feel that they have made the wrong decision. Do not argue with the judge. It you think the decision is wrong discuss this with your lawyers who will be able to advise on the merits of appealing the decision.

On-the-spot questions	1 Reflecting on cases you/your colleagues have been involved in, what are your impressions of judges? 2 What did they do well? 3 What could they have done better? 4 How should this affect, if at all, your approach to courts in future?

What is evidence?

Judges (or juries in the case of jury trials) must weigh up the evidence before coming to their decision. Evidence may be oral (from the witness 'live' in court, over a **live-link** closed circuit TV or even over a Skype connection if the witness is overseas) or written in the form of a report or a statement. If the written evidence is disputed (not accepted) by the other side, then usually the witness must be called. If that is not possible, the judge might allow the evidence to be introduced anyway but the fact that the witness was not available to be cross-examined is likely to have a bearing on the weight that is attached to their evidence.

Judges have to put boundaries on how much evidence is called for in a particular case. They do this by only allowing evidence if it is relevant and when witnesses are called they can set time limits on how long they can be cross-examined for. In addition to hearing from witnesses or reading their written evidence, the courts can consider other types of evidence such as computer records, photographs etc.

The **burden of proof** refers to the responsibility of the person or organization bringing the case to prove what they are alleging. Who carries it?

Civil courts	usually carried by the party bringing the case i.e. the **claimant**
Family Courts	usually carried by the party bringing the case i.e. the local authority or the **applicant**
Criminal courts	usually carried by the party bringing the case i.e. the Crown

Table 1.2: The burden of proof

The **standard of proof** is the degree to which a case must be proved by the party with the burden of proof. What is the standard?

Civil courts	on the balance of probability
Family Courts	on the balance of probability
Criminal courts	beyond reasonable doubt

Table 1.3: The standard of proof

> **KEY CASE ANALYSIS**

R v Cannings [2004]

This case concerned a mother's successful appeal against convictions for murdering two of her children. New expert evidence relating to research into sudden infant death syndrome (SIDS) came to light after the trial. The convictions were found by the Court of Appeal to be unsafe and they were quashed. This case came in the wake of another well-publicized SIDS case about the wrongful conviction of a mother for murdering her two young baby boys (*R v Clark* [2003]).

In *Cannings*, the Court of Appeal stated that in a criminal case:

> it is simply not enough to be able to establish even a high probability of guilt. Unless we are sure of guilt the dreadful possibility always remains that a mother, already brutally scarred by the unexplained death or deaths of her babies, may find herself in prison for life for killing them when she should not be there at all. In our community, and in any civilized community, that is abhorrent. [179]

Thus we are reminded that the burden of proof is on the prosecution to prove guilt beyond reasonable doubt. It is not for the defendant to prove their innocence.

Care proceedings are a civil matter and the standard of proof is the civil standard – the balance of probability – however, the burden rests on the local authority to prove its case and, again, the parents are not obliged to prove anything.

Some of the courts and tribunals that you might appear in

Criminal courts

- Youth Court
- Magistrates' Court
- Crown Court

Family Courts and the Court of Protection

- Family Proceedings Court*
- Care Centre*
- Principal Registry of the Family Division*
- High Court (Family Division)*
- Court of Protection

The Crime and Courts Act 2013 brought in new legislation to establish a single Family Court for England and Wales. In 2014, the Family Courts (those marked with an asterisk in the above list) will be reorganized to become 'unified' into one Family Court. The High Court will still remain and deal with what is likely to be a relatively small proportion of applications in respect of children (such as wardship and international cases) and applications in respect of incapacitated or vulnerable adults.

Civil courts

- County Court
- High Court

Tribunals

- Employment Tribunal
- Mental Health Review Tribunal
- Immigration and Asylum Tribunal
- SENDIST

Others

- fitness-to-practise hearings
- public inquires
- Coroner's Court

On-the-spot questions	1 Have you or your colleagues ever appeared in any of the courts above? 2 In which courts is the 'balance of probability' the usual standard of proof? 3 In which courts is it 'beyond reasonable doubt'?

Further reading

There are many books on the English legal system. The texts cited below are a good starting point for social workers.

Brammer, A (2011) 'Law and social work' in Wilson et al. is a social work-specific guide to the law.

Darbyshire, P (2013) *Nutshells: English Legal System* is a nutshell guide setting out fundamentals.

Laming, Lord (2003) *The Victoria Climbié Inquiry*: every social worker should be familiar with the facts and the key findings of Lord Laming's report

2

RECORD-KEEPING AND HANDLING PERSONAL INFORMATION

AT A GLANCE THIS CHAPTER COVERS:

+ how records can make or break a legal case
+ what the Climbié, Soham and other inquiries can teach us about record-keeping and information-sharing
+ legal requirements when handling personal data
+ keeping data safe
+ handling requests for information
+ what opposing lawyers look for
+ chapter summary checklist

How records can make or break a case

The primary purpose of social work records is to assist you in decision-making. The secondary purpose is to help resolve a dispute if one arises. Was the referral made? What support was the foster carer promised? How often were visits agreed? And so on. If the matter goes to court, records may be used in two ways: to establish the 'history' of the case and/or to judge the quality of the social work.

The records you keep as a social worker are always going to be of significance to lawyers if you seek their advice and especially if the case goes to court. It is impossible to know in advance which of the case files that you keep during your career will one day be scrutinized by lawyers/the court; it follows that every record should be kept to the best of your ability.

During your training and through work experience you will have been taught skills for record-keeping and websites such as the Social Care Institute for Excellence give advice on form-filling, case notes and taking minutes of meetings, for example. Each organization will have its own system for making and keeping records; increasingly record-keeping methods are becoming electronic but you will also need to use your judgement to decide which and how much information to record.

You should follow the record-keeping guidance given by your organization but in addition note that the law requires personal information to be recorded, stored and shared with care.

The third and fourth principles of the Data Protection Act 1998 tell us that:

3 Personal data shall be adequate, relevant and not excessive in relation to the purpose or purposes for which they are processed.
4 Personal data shall be accurate and, where necessary, kept up to date.

Part I, Schedule 1 Data Protection Act 1998

Case file chronologies are an essential part of record-keeping. There are several ways to create chronologies, from the handwritten A4 file note on the top of the paper file to the computer-generated one in your electronic case notes. Every file should have one. This has been the law since the judgment of Bracewell J in the case of *Re E and Others (Minors) (Care Proceedings: Social Work Practice)* [2000].

It is up to you to make the chronology a useful document that:

- you can turn to quickly to remind yourself of the relevant history;
- you can easily convert into a chronology for court proceedings if required; and
- a colleague (if you are on leave/move on) can look at and quickly appreciate important events in that service user's history.

All this requires dates and details of key events to be recorded and, where appropriate, chronology entries to be cross-referenced to other information on the file.

For example, if you have concerns about a mother's engagement with you and their child's non-attendance at school you will know that you will need to record information relevant to those issues so entries might look at follows:

4 Sept 2013	Called Mrs Bloggs, confirmed home visit following Monday at 11am
6 Sept 2013	Sunny High School report Joe has not been at school this term (see email from headteacher)
9 Sept 2013	11 am home visit attempted – no response
12 Sept 2013	Mr Bloggs attended office and disclosed concerns re Joe (see file note)

In respect of the last but one entry, your file note would probably contain details such as 'at 10:55, rang bell twice, waited for 10 minutes, no reply'. In respect of the last entry above, your file note should record, as precisely as possible, the words that he used since this information may prove to be highly significant in any future legal proceedings. You may even wish to make a note and ask Mr Bloggs to read over it and sign it to confirm it is an accurate record of what he said.

Usually, formal documents for court (statements or reports) are drafted months, years or even decades after the events took place. You will be relying on your records to provide a truthful and accurate account of what happened; ensure that what you write is going to make sense to you and others months or years later. In the example above, for 13 September 2013, if you had just written 'CHV' because that was your idiosyncratic abbreviation for 'confirmed home visit', others or even you sometime later might not know what it meant. (Could it be 'called health visitor'?). Nor would it be helpful help if you had not specified in your records the time and the date of your proposed home visit if Mrs Bloggs was later contending that you had in fact told her you were coming on *Tuesday* at 11.

> **KEY CASE ANALYSIS**

Kirsty X v Oldham Metropolitan Borough Council [2013]

In this case, a young woman, aged 25, brought a claim for damages against the local authority, alleging breaches of the duty of care owed to her by the social services department when she was a child, including negligent delay in taking her into care and failure to provide her with therapy.

The judge said:

> [t]o test whether [the social worker made a negligent mistake], I have carefully considered the contemporaneous records. Such records provide, in my judgment, the best evidence of how the decision making was approached at the time and is the closest the court can come to assessing the decision on the basis of the circumstances existing when it was made rather than by applying hindsight. [38]

This case illustrates that, when a court is trying to determine what happened in the past, judges pay particular consideration to 'the contemporaneous records'. In this case these records from many years earlier were the key to determining the case.

'Contemporaneous records', that is those made at the time or as soon as possible after the event, are generally regarded as having greater evidential value than records made some time later when the witness's memory has had a chance to fade. Because of the evidential value placed on contemporaneous records, opposing lawyers will scrutinize records to see if there is anything to suggest that the records are unreliable, such as missing entries, unattributed entries or quotes, inaccuracies, a significant delay between the event and when the record was made etc.

Written records should indicate:

- who made the entry in the record;
- when the record was made – time and date;
- if the record refers to someone other than the author, who that person is;
- if other information is relied on, what it is and where it came from;
- if people are quoted, exactly who said what and when (if it is an exact quotation it should be in speech marks);

- if the record is incomplete, why it is incomplete – do not gloss over or try to cover up the fact that an entry is missing or information was not available;
- details of the interpreter used, if any (if the service user's first language is not English and no interpreter is used, the record should say why not);
- details of any communications aids or assistance used, for example, if you were relying on Makaton signing.

It is important to comply with your organization's record-keeping and file management procedures and comply with the legal requirement to keep adequate, relevant and not excessive, accurate and up-to-date records. You should be prepared to have your case records inspected by management on a regular basis. Lord Laming said that:

> Directors of social services must ensure that senior managers inspect, at least once every three months, a random selection of case files and supervision notes. (Climbié report, Recommendation 30, Laming, 2003)

It is good professional development practice to ask your manager or one of your experienced colleagues to regularly review your case notes and give you feedback on your records and chronologies.

It is acknowledged that computer systems may not be as effective as you would like or need them to be. A recent inquiry reported widespread dissatisfaction with the information technology systems available to social workers. The *Inquiry into the State of Social Work* (All Party Parliamentary Group on Social Work, 2013) found that systems ought to be overhauled so as to move away from 'over-structured data keeping' to records which explain the child's circumstances. If you do not keep good case records and chronologies it may subsequently be argued at court that your practice was 'sloppy' and the court might decide that it cannot place much or any reliance on your evidence. This could adversely affect the outcome of the case and your professional reputation.

When professional witnesses such as social workers, nurses and police officers draft witness statements, the starting point will be their records. The following court case powerfully illustrates the importance of record-keeping. The court was asked to determine whether or not serious sexual abuse allegations were true. What was recorded when the allegations were first made was of crucial importance. The court found the 'documentary trail' to be 'of considerable evidential importance'.

Re A (A Child) (Vulnerable Witness: Fact Finding) [2013]

In this case, the judge needed to determine whether serious sexual allegations made against the father of a child (A) were true or not. The allegations had been made by the father's niece, X, a very vulnerable 17.5-year-old girl. X had not made a statement to the police in the usual way nor had she been video-interviewed by the police. The importance of the records of a number of key individuals to whom she had disclosed information were therefore of the utmost importance.

The judge was able to conclude that the social workers and police who undertook inquiries 'were well-versed and trained in child protection' and their records were 'carefully made' and that there were 'significant additions to the documents from both the school and the voluntary organisation'. The records provided 'a documentary trail from a variety of reliable sources as to what was said'.

On-the-spot questions

1 Thinking about your own files, do they always have a chronology?
2 If you went back to your files in one year/five years, how much sense would they make to you or to others?

What the Climbié, Soham and other inquiries can teach us about record-keeping and information-sharing

Lord Laming's report into the death of Victoria Climbié was published in January 2003 and poor record-keeping and inadequate information-sharing were recurring features of the case. It was necessary for the inquiry chair Lord Laming to include the following as one of the top priorities:

Front-line staff in each of the agencies which regularly come into contact with families with children must ensure that in each new contact, basic information about the child is recorded. This must include the child's name, address, age, the name of the child's primary carer, the child's GP, and the name of the child's school if the child is of school age.

Recommendation 12, Climbié report, Laming, 2003

Even if social work records are well kept, problems arise if professionals do not share information with each other when they need to. Lord Laming concluded that professionals would be assisted by clear guidance on confidentiality and the exchange of information. He made the following recommendation:

> The government should issue guidance on the Data Protection Act 1998, the Human Rights Act 1998, and common law rules on confidentiality. The government should issue guidance as and when these impact on the sharing of information between professional groups in circumstances where there are concerns about the welfare of children and families.
>
> *Recommendation 16, Climbié report, Laming, 2003*

In 2004, Sir Michael Bichard led an inquiry into child protection procedures in light of the trial and conviction of Ian Huntley for the murders of Jessica Chapman and Holly Wells. Sir Michael Bichard's report said:

> ... better guidance is needed on the collection, retention, deletion, use and sharing of information, so that police officers, social workers and other professionals can feel more confident in using information properly (Bichard, 2004: 'Introduction and summary', para. 23).

In 2004, Sir Christopher Kelly's serious case review looked at how well the statutory agencies in North East Lincolnshire responded to the individual needs of the young people known to them who had contact with Ian Huntley. Record-keeping and information-sharing were highlighted as significant problem areas. Sir Christopher Kelly's report stated:

> It is easy to understand how record keeping can suffer when people are working under pressure. But good record keeping is not just a matter of bureaucracy. Data which are not recorded properly, or which are scattered across innumerable files on scrappy pieces of paper, are not information. Continuity can be lost; and supervision and information sharing both become much more difficult. Poor record keeping can also be symptomatic of a sloppy approach to case handling.
>
> *Kelly, 2004: para. 201*

If the information recorded on the files is inaccurate or incomplete then clearly the information shared is going to be at best unhelpful and at worst misleading. In 2006 the government published *Information Sharing: Guidance for Practitioners and Managers* which was modified slightly and published as an updated version in 2008.

Information Sharing: Guidance for Practitioners and Managers (DCSF, 2008) states:

> Information sharing is key to the Government's goal of delivering better, more efficient public services that are coordinated around the needs of the individual. It is essential to enable early intervention and preventative work, for safeguarding and promoting welfare and for wider public protection. Information sharing is a vital element in improving outcomes for all. [1.1]
>
> Practitioners recognise the importance of information sharing and there is already much good practice. However, in some situations they feel constrained from sharing information by uncertainty about when they can do so lawfully, especially in early intervention and preventative work where information sharing decisions may be less clear than in safeguarding or child protection situations. For those who have to make decisions about information sharing on a case-by-case basis, this document seeks to give clear practical guidance, drawing on experience and consultation from across a spectrum of adult and children's services. [1.3]
>
> *DCSF, 2008*

Following the case of 'Baby P', Lord Laming provided a progress report on safeguarding children (*The Protection of Children in England: A Progress Report*) which found that information-sharing was still not well understood.

> 4.6 Despite the fact that the Government gave clear guidance on information sharing in 2006 and updated it in October 2008, there continues to be a real concern across all sectors, but particularly in the health services, about the risk of breaching confidentiality or data protection law by sharing concerns about a child's safety. The laws governing data protection and privacy are still not well understood by frontline staff or their managers. It is clear that different agencies (and their legal advisers) often take different approaches.
>
> 4.7 Whilst the law rightly seeks to preserve individuals' privacy and confidentiality, it should not be used (and was never intended) as a

barrier to appropriate information sharing between professionals. The safety and welfare of children is of paramount importance, and agencies may lawfully share confidential information about the child or the parent, without consent, if doing so is in the public interest. A public interest can arise in a wide range of circumstances, including the protection of a child from harm, and the promotion of child welfare. Even where the sharing of confidential medical information is considered inappropriate, it may be proportionate for a clinician to share the fact that they have concerns about a child.

Laming, 2009

In March 2013, the government responded to Lord Carlile's report on the Edlington case. Lord Carlile had said that '[t]ime and again, poor information sharing between practitioners has been highlighted in [Serious Case Reviews]' (2012). The government said that:

... revised statutory guidance *Working Together* [2013] makes clear that misplaced fears about sharing information cannot be allowed to stand in the way of the need to safeguard and promote the welfare of children. Effective information sharing between agencies and among practitioners is critical to providing early help when problems are emerging and is essential for effective child protection.

DfE, 2013

The Information-Sharing Guidance (DCSF, 2008), though created in response to child protection concerns, is relevant in all situations where you wish to share personal data about individuals. It is just as relevant to safeguarding vulnerable adults as it is to child protection.

Legal requirements when handling personal data

The starting point is to recognize that confidentiality is at the heart of a relationship of trust between the social worker and the service user but no social worker can or should ever promise absolute confidentiality in the sense of a promise never to pass on information. If a service user thought that their personal information was going to be shared any old how, without restriction, they would probably not be open about their situation or concerns. However, it is necessary sometimes to share service users' personal information to obtain support for them or to protect them or others.

The service user needs to know that there is no such thing as 'absolute confidentiality'. It is something that should always be discussed with the service user when they first engage with the service. Some organizations will provide leaflets to explain this and the social worker may have it listed as a point to cover when they first open the file and meet the service user. Unfortunately, various inquiries have shown that many professionals find information-sharing and confidentiality tricky to understand and explain – the law is a hotch-potch and this adds to people's nervousness.

Timothy Pitt-Payne QC, a barrister specializing in information law, said:

> [d]ata protection is not a popular subject, even among lawyers. Most of us have been refused an answer to some innocuous question 'because of data protection'. The Data Protection Act 1998 is badly drafted and obscure ... Nevertheless the subject is inescapable. (Pitt-Payne, 2013)

Luckily you do not need to learn the data laws, nor do you need to be in a fog of confusion. *Information Sharing: Guidance for Practitioners and Managers* (DCSF, 2008) contains what you need to know. The Information-Sharing Guidance is less than 40 pages long; it explains the law in plain English and shows how the law underpins the guidance. A succinct flowchart walks the practitioner through key questions when determining whether or not to share information.

The guidance explains that the Human Rights Act 1998, the common law (judge-made law), duty of confidentiality and the Data Protection Act 1998 each play a part in protecting an individual's right to privacy and the confidentiality of their personal data. However, none of these legal rights is absolute; there are exceptions. The law is a 'framework not a barrier' to information-sharing.

What it amounts to (in the briefest of nutshells) is that confidential information about an individual must not be 'processed' (this includes sharing) unless either (i) that person has given their consent, or (ii) the law requires the information to be shared e.g. because there is a court order to do so or a specific requirement in legislation that says it must be shared, or (iii) sharing in the 'public interest' is justifiable.

Official guidance for practitioners and managers

The 'seven golden rules' (taken from *Information Sharing: Guidance for Practitioners and Managers* (DCSF, 2008)) and the following questions 1–7 will help support your decision-making so you can be more confident that information is being shared legally and professionally. If you answer 'not sure' to any of the questions, seek advice from your supervisor, manager, nominated person within your organization or area, or from a professional body.

Question 1: is there a clear and legitimate purpose for sharing information?

Why do you or the other person want the information? What is the outcome you are trying to achieve? Could the aims be achieved without sharing the information?

Question 2: does the information enable a living person to be identified?

If the information is about an identifiable living individual, or could enable a living person to be identified when considered with other information, it is personal information and is subject to data protection law. This is likely to be the case in the course of your work. You should be open about what information you might need to share and why. However, it may not be appropriate to inform a person that information is being shared, or seek consent to this sharing. This is the case if informing them is likely to hamper the prevention or investigation of a serious crime, or put a child at risk of significant harm, or an adult at risk of serious harm.

Question 3: is the information confidential?

Not all information is confidential. Confidential information is information of a private or sensitive nature that is: not already lawfully in the public domain or readily available from another public source; and has been provided in circumstances where the person giving the information could reasonably expect that it would not be shared with others.

Question 4: do you have consent to share?

You should seek consent where possible and respect the wishes of those who do not consent to share confidential information. You may still share information without consent if, in your judgement on the facts of the case, that lack of consent can be overridden in the public interest. You do not always need consent to share personal information. There will be some circumstances where you should not seek consent, for example, where doing so would: place a child at increased risk of significant harm; or place an adult at increased risk of serious harm; or prejudice the prevention, detection or prosecution of a serious crime; or lead to unjustified delay in making enquiries about allegations of significant harm or serious harm.

Question 5: is there sufficient public interest to share the information?

Even where you do not have consent to share confidential information, you may lawfully share it if this can be justified in the public interest. Where consent cannot be obtained or is refused, or where seeking it is unsafe or inappropriate (as explained at Question 4), the question of whether there is a sufficient public interest must be judged by the practitioner on the facts of each case. A public interest can arise in a wide range of circumstances. For a fuller definition of public interest refer to the glossary in *Information Sharing: Guidance for Practitioners and Managers* (DCSF, 2008). Where you have a concern about a person, you should not regard refusal of consent as necessarily to mean that you cannot share confidential information. In making the decision you must weigh up what might happen if the information is shared against what might happen if it is not, and make a decision based on professional judgement.

Question 6: are you sharing information appropriately and securely?

Only share what is necessary to achieve the purpose, distinguishing clearly between fact and opinion. Share only with the person or people who really need to know the information. Make sure the information is accurate and up to date. Understand the limits of any consent given, especially if the information has been provided by a third party. Check who will see the information and share the information in a secure way. For example, confirm the identity of the person you are talking to; ensure a conversation or phone call cannot be overheard; use secure email; ensure that the intended person will be on hand to receive a fax. Establish with the recipient whether they intend to pass it on to other people and ensure that they understand the limits of any consent that has been given. Inform the person to whom the information relates that you are sharing the information, if it is safe to do so, and if you have not already told them that their information may be shared.

Question 7: have you properly recorded your information-sharing decision?

Record your information-sharing decision and your reasons, including what information you have shared and with whom, following your agency's arrangements for recording information and in line with any local information-sharing procedures in place. If, at any stage, you decide not to share information, you should record this decision and the reasons for it.

Remember the Information-Sharing Guidance is not just for social workers. It is for police, nurses, doctors, teachers and other professionals. The law applies to us all.

PRACTICE FOCUS

Imagine that you wish to obtain information from the GP of a young child (to whom you are the allocated social worker) for the purposes of a child safeguarding enquiry. The practice manager at the GP's surgery says that the child's doctor 'will not release information without the mother's consent'. You know that she will not give you that consent.

• Can the doctor release the information to you anyway and, if so, on what legal basis?

In addition to the flowchart in the Information Sharing Guidance, seven golden rules are set out. The guidance should, however, be read in full.

Seven golden rules for information-sharing

1 Remember that the Data Protection Act is not a barrier to sharing information but provides a framework to ensure that personal information about living persons is shared appropriately.
2 Be open and honest with the person (and/or their family where appropriate) from the outset about why, what, how and with whom information will, or could be shared, and seek their agreement, unless it is unsafe or inappropriate to do so.
3 Seek advice if you are in any doubt, without disclosing the identity of the person where possible.
4 Share with consent where appropriate and, where possible, respect the wishes of those who do not consent to share confidential information. You may still share information without consent if, in your judgement, that lack of consent can be overridden in the public interest. You will need to base your judgement on the facts of the case.

> 5 **Consider safety and well-being:** Base your information sharing deci-
> sions on considerations of the safety and well-being of the person and
> others who may be affected by their actions.
> 6 **Necessary, proportionate, relevant, accurate, timely and secure:**
> Ensure that the information you share is necessary for the purpose for
> which you are sharing it, is shared only with those people who need
> to have it, is accurate and up-to-date, is shared in a timely fashion,
> and is shared securely.
> 7 **Keep a record** of your decision and the reasons for it – whether it is
> to share information or not. If you decide to share, then record what
> you have shared, with whom and for what purpose.
>
> *DCSF, 2008*

Sometimes the decision to share or not to share creates such an acute
issue for the local authority that the court's decision is sought. *In the
matter of A (A Child)* [2012] was one such case. The facts illustrate the
balance which has to be struck between an individual's right to confidentiality and the necessity to share information. X, the vulnerable witness,
did not want her identity to be disclosed to the father involved in a child
contact dispute. X had made very serious allegations concerning the

PRACTICE FOCUS

Imagine you are the social worker to Jimmy who is 19. Jimmy has
cerebral palsy and lives with his mother Jane, his sole carer. Jane has
commenced a course at university to train to be a social worker. You
are concerned about Jane's fitness to be a social worker because she
has anger management issues. Jane has hit Jimmy twice in the last
three years and Jimmy has twice been placed in respite care as a result.
Jane refuses to take part in individual therapy and blames Jimmy. You
are considering writing a short letter to Jane's university explaining
the history in brief. If you do, you are aware that the university is
likely to hold an inquiry, giving Jane a chance to explain. It is possible that it may remove Jane from the course after conducting its own
inquiry. You know from previous conversations that Jane would not
agree to you writing to the university.

- Should you share information with the university?
- If you do, should you tell Jane first?
- What questions does the guidance say you should be asking yourself?

father but she had made them in confidence to the local authority social worker. The court felt on balance that her identity had to be disclosed to allow the father to have a fair hearing. Each court decision is based on the facts in the particular case. No two cases will be exactly the same. Each decision is a careful balancing exercise.

Social workers don't usually have the luxury of going to court to ask the court to determine the correct decision when there is an information-sharing dilemma. The Information-Sharing Guidance (DCSF, 2008) is there to help you and so are your colleagues, including your line manager, legal advisers and information officers. Follow the information-sharing guidance (including the decision-making flowchart containing the seven key questions) and make a note in your records of whom you consulted, the guidance you followed, what you decided and why. There is not always just one right answer; there may be more than one reasonable course of action. You are required to make a reasonable decision by applying the guidance to the facts. Then document it. Dickens summed it up as follows:

> The virtuous person shares what is necessary in the interests of the service user and wider society, but the challenge is to know what the mid-point is between indiscretion and reticence. (Dickens, 2013)

PRACTICE FOCUS

Imagine you are the local authority social worker to a two-year-old girl, Angel. She has been placed by you with local authority-approved foster carers under an interim care order because her mother's alcohol dependence and chaotic lifestyle were putting Angel at risk. You are assessing the child's father and his new partner as carers. You have now discovered that the foster father is HIV positive. The foster father objects to that information being passed on to Angel's parents.

- Can you disclose the foster father's HIV status without his consent?
- Whom, if anyone, should you inform?

The above practice-focused case study idea was inspired by *London Borough of Brent v N and Others* [2005]. It is a relatively short judgment (36 paragraphs) and demonstrates a judge making a decision based on the facts of the case and requiring a consideration of the foster father's rights to privacy as well as what, if anything, would be achieved by disclosing the information to the child's father and his partner. The judgment gives several examples of other cases concerning, for example, the disclosure of a person's convictions as a paedophile and, in another, the publication of the HIV status of doctors.

It cannot be over-emphasized that cases depend on their own set of facts. Each case is different from the next and there is no handbook to which you can turn that will give you the answer to your particular dilemma. What you can and should do is apply the Information-Sharing Guidance and consult with your manager/colleagues and legal advisers if in any doubt about the right approach. Use the flowchart and record your decision and the fact that you followed the 2008 guidance. The Information-Sharing Guidance poster with the decision-making flowchart should be up in your office. If you use it often enough it will become second nature and your decision-making will be systematic, focused and should stand up to legal scrutiny.

Keeping data safe

In 2008 the *Data Sharing Review Report* carried out by Dr Mark Walport of the Wellcome Trust and the Information Commissioner, Richard Thomas, said that:

> Repeated losses of sensitive personal information in both the public and private sectors demonstrate the weakness of many organisations in managing how data are shared. (Walport and Thomas, 2008:i)

The highest profile loss in recent years occurred at Her Majesty's Revenue and Customs where inadequate systems and procedures resulted in the loss of two unencrypted discs containing personal data of 25 million people.

The Information Commissioner's Office includes details of fines issued to public and private bodies for losses of personal data. For example, in June 2013 Glasgow City Council was issued with a monetary penalty notice for the loss of two unencrypted laptops, one of which contained the personal information of 20,143 people. The month before saw Halton Borough Council receive a monetary penalty notice in respect of an incident in which the home address of adoptive parents was wrongly disclosed to the birth family. In December 2012 there were two fines issued to councils for social work mistakes:

> a social worker left sensitive documents in a plastic shopping bag on a train, after taking them home to work on. The files, which were later recovered from the rail company's lost property office, included GP and police reports and allegations of sexual abuse and neglect.

In another council:

> a social worker used a previous case as a template for an adoption panel report they were writing, but a copy of the old report was sent out instead of the new one. The mistake revealed personal data of 22 people, including details of alleged criminal offences and mental and physical health.

These examples and more can be found on the website of the Information Commissioner's Office: http://ico.org.uk.

If you type in your local authority's name in the search engine does anything come up?

Inquiry reports, case law and these recent examples repeatedly underline the importance of record-keeping, treating personal information with care and sharing information only when it is right to do so.

The emphasis in the Information-Sharing Guidance (DCSF, 2008) is on handling data correctly: respecting service user's rights to privacy and sharing where necessary to ensure the best outcomes for service users. In addition to damage that might result to individuals if data is mishandled, it can also lead to serious professional consequences for the social worker. In 2011 newspapers reported that a social worker from the Vale of Glamorgan was found guilty of misconduct by the Care Council of Wales conduct committee: a 19-year-old boy was placed with a foster family but the foster carers were not warned of his history of inappropriate sexual behaviour. The 19-year-old went on to seriously sexually assault the foster carer's two young children. The social worker had not read the case file properly, had not prepared an appropriate chronology and had not shared the necessary information with the foster carers.

The government's 2013 response to Lord Carlile's 'Edlington' report also acknowledged the importance of multi-agency information-sharing training (DfE, 2013). Training will provide you with a framework but each case will be different and, if you are in any doubt about what to do, you should consult your line manager and, if necessary, also the person in your organization tasked with providing advice on data-handling issues. The appropriate officer might be called the 'data controller', 'information manager', 'Caldicott guardian' or another title. You might also have access to legal advisers. Find out how to contact these people should you need advice. Make a note of the details on your information-sharing poster. Seek advice if you come across a situation you are unsure about.

Handling requests for information

When someone asks for information about another person you should follow the Information-Sharing Guidance to determine what, if any, information you should share. It should make no difference how much power or influence that person is perceived to have; requests from MPs, councillors, police officers etc. should all be dealt with like any other in accordance with the Information-Sharing Guidance (DCSF, 2008).

If an individual asks to know what information is held on file about themselves this is known as a 'subject access request' (s. 7 Data Protection Act 1984 gives individuals the right to access the personal information that an organization holds about them). Usually, the request should be dealt with within 40 calendar days of receipt. The Information Commissioner's Office website provides good advice but you should always ensure that these requests are directed to the appropriate data/information officer in your organization.

People also have the right to request information from a public authority under the Freedom of Information Act 2000 and such requests must be in writing but do not have to mention the Act or ask any particular member of staff. You might be the recipient of a request that is not even in your work area, however, you should inform your line manager and ensure that the request is dealt with by the appropriate person. Usually, the request should be dealt with within 20 working days of receipt. The Act does not provide a means of getting confidential data about individuals. Again, the Information Commissioner's Office website provides good advice and a decision-making flowchart but you should always ensure that these 'FOI' requests are directed to the appropriate officer in your organization.

If information is requested that is linked to a current or past court case or legal matter you should always consult your legal advisers. For example, a defence solicitor representing a service user accused of rape by 'the complainant' might ask for disclosure of information held on file about that complainant. Ask them to direct the request to the legal department and also contact your legal department as you should forewarn the legal department that the request is likely to be forthcoming. The defence solicitors might, for example, be after evidence on a social work file of an earlier, possibly false, allegation by the complainant that was later retracted or they might be making a speculative search, generally known as a 'fishing expedition'. Your legal advisers will liaise with the parties and the court. On the one hand, all the relevant information must be before the court to ensure that there is a fair trial, however, public interest immunity will be argued by the local authority i.e. that the records should be immune from disclosure because they are social work files and by their nature are confidential. It will be for the judge to determine, having inspected the file, the relevance of the information in it and whether or not it should be disclosed to the defence. The judge will balance the request for confidentiality against the need to have the information available for a fair trial. The social worker responsible for the files may need to attend court (and possibly carry the files there too) to assist at the hearing.

For cases involving children, such as care proceedings, or when children are witnesses or defendants in serious criminal cases, you should always be very conscious that there are likely to be special restrictions on what information can be shared, especially about the identities of people involved. Seek advice from your lawyers. In addition, press queries should be handled by your press officer and lawyers together.

What opposing lawyers look for

When social work records are disclosed to opposing lawyers they will be scrutinized. Opposing lawyers will check to see if the records support or undermine what you are saying or to assist their client's case. Below is a list of things that they will be on the look-out for. The list describes common mistakes that must be avoided *at the time* the record is made. This list could be utilized by the manager/colleague who peer-reviews your case records and gives you feedback on how well they are being kept.

| *On-the-spot question* | If an opposing lawyer went through your files, what would they think of your record-keeping skills? |

Written records should *not* have:

- missing or inaccurate 'basic data', such as names, dates of birth and addresses;
- an inadequate (or completely missing) chronology;
- 'lost' pages or entries;
- notes that are ambiguous, vague or open to interpretation (e.g. rather than 'he arrived approximately on time' or 'the house looked fairly tidy', say when he arrived and describe what you saw if these things are relevant);
- fact and opinion muddled – the record should be clear which is which;
- inappropriate comments about anyone (e.g. 'Dave acting like an idiot again');
- opinions noted without attributing the sources, especially for medical diagnoses (e.g. 'Fiona is depressed' or 'Connor has ADHD');
- conclusions not supported by the facts;
- opinions that are not justified, for example, because the author does not have the necessary expertise/qualifications to make that judgement;
- breaches of confidentiality;
- failure to share information as necessary;
- failure to record the decisions to share/not to share information.

Cover-ups, such as altering, withholding or deleting a record or part of one when it is required by lawyers or the court, are unethical, unprofessional and could land you in the dock of a criminal court.

There are six simple steps that you can take to ensure that you handle personal information well and that your records will withstand scrutiny.

Checklist for handling personal information

> ✓ Read *Information Sharing: Guidance for Practitioners and Managers* (DCSF, 2008).
> ✓ Print the poster of the seven golden rules and information-sharing flowchart and display it prominently in the office so it is on hand to help guide your decisions.
> ✓ Attend training (ideally multi-agency) on information-sharing and data protection.
> ✓ Make sure every file has an up-to-date chronology.
> ✓ Make sure records are adequate, relevant, not excessive in relation to the purpose, accurate and up to date.
> ✓ Obtain peer-review feedback on your record-keeping.

Further reading

DCSF (2008) *Information Sharing: Guidance for Practitioners and Managers*: this guidance book is quite simply a must-read. It applies to social workers in all fields and explains how to share information lawfully and in a way that is most likely to ensure that trust is maintained with service users and early, co-ordinated interventions take place.

Two other books for social workers also have very useful chapters on this subject:

Brayne, H and H Carr (2013) *Law for Social Workers*: in particular see chapter 4 'Information sharing'.

Dickens, J (2013) *Social Work, Law and Ethics*: in particular see chapter 12 'Confidentiality, information-sharing and openness'.

3

PRODUCING WRITTEN EVIDENCE

AT A GLANCE THIS CHAPTER COVERS:

- key principles for written evidence for criminal, civil and Family Courts
- pre-proceedings work
- objectivity and respectfulness
- principles and points on style
- what you need to know *before* you start writing
- statement and reports
- chronologies
- care plans

Key principles for written evidence for criminal, civil and Family Courts

Many cases that are contemplated or even started never actually get to court. This is because decisions about whether or not to proceed with or to defend a case are made after evaluation of the evidence. It is therefore vital that the written evidence is produced with the highest possible skill and care. It can and often does make or break a case even before it gets to court. However, if the matter does go to court and you give evidence, your work will be exposed to scrutiny by the cross-examiner, the judge and, if there is one, the jury as well. This chapter is all about how to prepare written evidence that will help not hinder the case and that will assist you if you give evidence.

If you invest time in your written evidence it will pay off. The more accurate and balanced it is the more you increase the chance that your evidence (or at least parts of it) will be accepted and you will not be challenged on it. If some of your written evidence is disputed you will be called as a witness.

To whom, by when and for what purpose?

If you are contemplating providing a draft statement for a legal case you need to know to whom you are supplying it, when they need it by and for what purpose. Sometimes this will be obvious, e.g. a decision has been made to start care proceedings. Specific guidance for care proceedings statements is dealt with below. Sometimes it is not so obvious, e.g. imagine you are approached by a private firm of solicitors asking for a witness statement from you to help them defend their client who is charged with assaulting a foster carer? Or suppose the police contact you in order to request a statement to support a prosecution against a parent for child neglect? Contact your legal advisers to make sure that they know about the request. It is likely that they will wish to be the 'conduit' for the two-way communication between the social worker and the solicitors/police/others, as the case may be. This allows your employer to keep a record of your involvement and to check your draft statement. Before you send it to the lawyers ask your manager to proofread it and give you feedback. You should never be asked to change your draft to distort the facts as you see them but a careful checking of the statement by your manager and the lawyer should help weed out typographical errors and identify incomplete information.

Once you have agreed a deadline by which you must supply your draft, stick to it. It is safe to assume that if the lawyer needs the statement by a certain date it is because there is a timetable to be adhered to. That timetable is usually set by the court and, if the statement is not filed in accordance with the timetable, a court order may be breached. Breaching a court order is a serious matter; the judge might take action and demand the lawyer and/or the social worker goes to court to explain the failure to comply. The judge might even make an order for payment of the wasted costs caused by the non-compliance.

Your voice, your words

It is an obvious but important point to make but the fact is that this is *your* statement, not the lawyer's, not the court's, not even the local authority's. You are the one who is signing a declaration to say that your written evidence is true. You are the one who may be asked to justify it or be challenged on it. Make sure that you know what you want to say, that you say it clearly and that are willing to stand by every single word in your statement.

Write it in your own words. There is no magic formula for this. Aim for short, clear sentences that are grammatically correct. Each and every person has their own way of expressing themselves. The words you use should be the ones that come naturally to you, not pseudo-legal or contrived expressions. As opposed to 'the writer then proceeded in a westerly direction towards the public house known as The Nag's Head whereupon she identified the male known as Billy Kidd' (an example admittedly exaggerated for effect), it would be better to write: 'I walked towards The Nag's Head pub and saw Billy Kidd outside.' Note it is written in the first person; it does not say 'the author did this' and 'the author did that'.

Try to avoid jargon. Is your audience going to understand it? For example, is 'referral pathway' a useful phrase or is it obscure language to the non-social worker?

The best evidence a court can get is from the person who was actually there at the time of the relevant event. Your statement should be about what you saw and did. If you find yourself including remarks about what others told you, it is important that you say who told you (the source) and what they told you (in the exact words if possible).

When your manager reviews your statement, if it contains social work recommendations, be prepared for differences of opinion. You will need to fully explore these differences with your manager, however, at the end of the day, the statement is yours and you must be prepared to stand by it. The judge in *A County Council v K and Others (by the Child's Guardian Ht)* [2011] said this:

> Usually, as has been said many times, the choice is between two more or less unsatisfactory answers ... In my judgment, there is nothing unhealthy or wrong about a disagreement between professionals in care proceedings. As I have already stated, there is frequently no unequivocally right answer in such cases. [103]

In the end you may have to agree to disagree with your manager about your evidence; you must say what you believe is true. You would be giving false evidence if you said something in evidence that you did not believe was true or took out something so as to give a misleading impression. Perjury (giving false evidence) is a criminal offence – no employer should ever ask that of an employee.

Sticking to the facts, as recorded

As has been discussed in Chapter 2, it is essential that you keep good records and that your statement faithfully represents what was recorded at the time, not 'some months later'. The judgment in *Re E (A Child)* [2013] included these words:

> In relation to statements for court proceedings it is essential they are based on contemporaneous records, not recollections made some months later. Repeatedly in this case witnesses when confronted with the contemporaneous records had to revise the contents of their written statements ... In addition, there is an obligation, particularly on public authorities who are seeking orders that interfere with Article 8 rights to family life, for a balanced picture to be presented, not just the negative information, or the facts cast only in a negative light.
>
> Re E (A Child) *[2013]:[78]*

The court is likely to take a dim view of a statement that appears to inflate, or exaggerate what is noted in the records. For example, this was said in *Re X (Emergency Protection Orders)* [2006]:

> The social worker's note reads: '[Nurse] stated Mother attended Walk-in with X with abdominal pain. Mother demanded further investigation, stating this was an ongoing problem. Worms for the last 2 years ... X referred to Children's A+E. Nurse's observation of X is that she is fine.' This note somehow became inflated when the social worker later produced her statement in support of the application for an interim care order to: 'Mother then demanded X have further investigations *and treatment*.'
>
> Re X (Emergency Protection Orders) *[2006]:[33]* (emphasis added)

Although these are examples from family cases, the general principle applies to all: your written evidence must be balanced and fair and based on your contemporaneous records.

If you and your legal advisers feel that it is important to put something in your statement that is not in the records it is important that you explain the source of the information and why it is not in your records. The court can then decide how much weight (if any) to attach to the information that was not recorded. It raises the question: if it really happened at the time and was relevant, why was it not recorded?

Stick to what you know and don't stray beyond that

If your evidence requires you to give an opinion based on your professional expertise, it is essential that you identify when a question falls

> ### → KEY CASE ANALYSIS ←
>
> *General Medical Council v Meadow* [2006]
>
> In *General Medical Council v Meadow* [2006], Professor Sir Roy Meadow was found to have been guilty of professional misconduct arising from the evidence he gave at the trial of Sally Clark. Professor Meadow's evidence had been relied on by the Prosecution to refute the claim that Mrs Clark's children may have died from SIDS, or cot death.
>
> Subsequently, Professor Meadow was brought before the General Medical Council Fitness to Practise Panel. He appealed the decision but the court concluded he was guilty of professional misconduct because he had strayed outside his area of expertise. Whilst this case involved a medical expert, the principle about not straying into giving opinion evidence if you are not qualified to speak on that topic applies to everyone.

outside your area of expertise. For example, if you are a child and family social worker you could give an opinion on the best interests of the child based on your review of the case; however, you would be straying outside your area of expertise if you were to offer an opinion based on hospital records about how an injury was inflicted. For this, it might be necessary to obtain expert medical advice.

Do not stray into giving opinions on topics you are not qualified to talk about. To do so could amount to professional misconduct even if you do so with the best intentions of helping the court.

Could a social worker be biased?

A social worker should be conscious of the fact that being on one side of adversarial litigation can lead to unconscious bias. Numerous studies have been carried out including one (Murrie et al., 2013) with 99 forensic scientists paid to measure the risks presented by sex offenders. The results of the experiment showed that the fact that they were instructed by either prosecution or defence in the experiment tended to influence their opinions.

A question that social workers can ask themselves as they reflect on their own recommendations is: if I had been asked the same questions by the other side would my answers have been exactly the same? If the answer is 'no' then there is a problem.

This question is a variation on the test described in the *Protocol for the Instruction of Experts to Give Evidence in Civil Claims*:

> Experts should provide opinions which are independent, regardless of the pressures of litigation. In this context, a useful test of 'independence' is that the expert would express the same opinion if given the same instructions by an opposing party. Experts should not take it upon themselves to promote the point of view of the party instructing them or engage in the role of advocates.
>
> *Civil Justice Council, 2005, amended 2009:[4.3]*

How to set out your statement

Your legal department should advise you on the format of your statement and the issues that it wants you to address. In some cases, the legal department will have a standard template with suggested headings that will guide you. There will also be a standard declaration that appears at the end of the statement and the wording depends on what sort of case it is.

A two-page statement in a criminal case would have this declaration on each page:

> This statement consisting of 2 pages signed by me is true to the best of my knowledge and belief and I make it, knowing that if it is tendered in evidence, I shall be liable to prosecution if I have wilfully stated in it anything which I know to be false or do not believe to be true.

In a civil case the declaration would usually be:

> I believe that the facts stated in this witness statement are true.

The statement should deal with the matters that are relevant to the court and be set out in a way that is helpful to the reader. In most cases, the social worker will be describing an incident or series of incidents. In some cases, such as care proceedings in the Family Court or adult safeguarding hearings in the Court of Protection, the social worker will also be required to give opinion on the welfare of their service users. The lawyers will be looking for a truthful description by the social worker of what he or she saw, heard or did. If an opinion is also called for, they will be looking for an evidence-based, well-reasoned conclusion.

It often makes logical sense, to the writer and the reader, to set out the facts chronologically. However, for a more complex, lengthier statement it might make more sense to deal with issues under separate headings. Your lawyer can advise you on the relevant issues and the best way to set out your evidence. The type of case it is and the social worker's role in it will influence the format of the statement.

There is generally very little official guidance on what goes into a statement (although the local authority legal department might keep templates or exemplars), however, this is not the case for applications for care or supervision orders under the Children Act 1989. Detailed guidance has been issued under a case management protocol called the Public Law Outline (PLO) (Practice Direction 12A). Social workers' documentation supplied in support of an application for a care or supervision order must comply with the PLO. (There is no PLO equivalent for the Court of Protection but this is something that is likely to change in the near future.)

Children Act applications and the Public Law Outline 2014: Practice Direction 12A

The PLO is a case management protocol; it sets out how the judges are expected to timetable cases and to oversee the key stages from start to finish. A new version of the PLO was issued in 2014 with the intention that it will support the implementation of a 26-week time limit for proceedings from the start (issue of the application) to finish (final order). The PLO also aims to promote early engagement of the parents with the local authority which is contemplating proceedings, better quality applications and more efficient court hearings.

The PLO pre-proceedings checklist specifies that an application form for a care or supervision order under the Children Act 1989 must be accompanied by the following:

1 social work chronology;
2 social work statement and genogram;
3 the current assessments relating to the child and/or the family and friends of the child to which the social work statement refers and on which the local authority relies;
4 care plan;
5 index of checklist documents (see below).

It will be the social worker's responsibility, supported by his or her manager, to draft (1) to (5).

The checklist documents will be derived from the social work records and the local authority lawyer will request the relevant documents from the social worker from the following list:

(a) Evidential documents including–
   • Previous court orders and judgments/reasons
   • Any assessment materials relevant to the key issues including Section 7 and 37 reports
   • Single, joint or inter-agency materials (e.g., health & education/Home Office and Immigration Tribunal documents);
(b) Decision-making records including–
   • Records of key discussions with the family
   • Key LA [local authority] minutes and records for the child
   • Pre-existing care plans (e.g., child in need plan, looked after child plan and child protection plan)
   • Letters Before Proceedings [this means any letter from the local authority containing written notification to the parents and others

with parental responsibility for the child of the local authority's plan to apply to court for a care or supervision order and any related subsequent correspondence confirming the Local Authority's position].

PD12A

The PLO states that 'Only Checklist documents in (a) are to be served with the application form' and documents in (b) are 'to be disclosed on request by any party'.

It also states that:

Checklist documents are not to be–
- filed with the court unless the court directs otherwise; and
- older than 2 years before the date of issue of the proceedings unless reliance is placed on the same in the LA's evidence.

PD12A

In summary: documents in (a) should go to the parties; documents in (b) should go to the parties if they request them; and documents in (a) and (b) should only go to the court if the court orders it. None of the documents in (a) or (b) should be older than two years before the date the proceedings were issued unless the local authority wants to use them in evidence.

It follows that, in order to comply with the requirements of the PLO when issuing an application, a social worker must be fully on top of the paperwork in the files and able to devote significant time to sorting the documentation and drafting a chronology for the court, their social work statement, a family genogram, and care plan(s) for the child/children.

The social work chronology means:

Annex 1 7.1

(a) a succinct summary of the significant dates and events in the child's life in chronological order – a running record up to the issue of the proceedings;
(b) information under the following headings –
    (i)   serial number;
    (ii) date;
    (iii) event-detail;
    (iv) witness or document reference (where applicable).

PD12A

The PLO outlines the headings of the social work statement:

Summary
(a) The order sought;
(b) Succinct summary of reasons with reference as appropriate to the Welfare Checklist;

Family
(c) Family members and relationships especially the primary carers and significant adults/other children;
(d) Genogram;

Threshold
(e) Precipitating events;
(f) Background circumstances;
      (i)   summary of children's services involvement cross-referenced to the chronology;
      (ii) previous court orders and emergency steps;
      (iii) previous assessments;
(g) Summary of significant harm and or likelihood of significant harm which the LA will seek to establish by evidence or concession;

Parenting capacity
(h) Assessment of child's needs;
(i) Assessment of parental capacity to meet needs;
(j) Analysis of why there is a gap between parental capacity and the child's needs;
(k) Assessment of other significant adults who may be carers;

Child impact
(l) Wishes and feelings of the child(ren);
(m) Timetable for the child;
(n) Delay and timetable for the proceedings;

Permanence and contact
(o) Parallel planning;
(p) Realistic placement options by reference to a welfare and proportionality analysis;
(q) Contact framework;

Case Management
(r) Evidence and assessments necessary and outstanding;
(s) Any information about any person's litigation capacity, mental health issues, disabilities or vulnerabilities that is relevant to their capability to participate in the proceedings; and
(t) Case management proposals.

PD12A

The President of the Family Division said in 2013:

> All too often, and partly as a result of previous initiatives, local authorities are filing enormously voluminous materials which – and this is not their fault – are not merely far too long; too often they are narrative and historical rather than analytical ... [local authority materials] should be more focused on analysis than on history and narrative.
>
> *Munby, 2013a:4*

Even where there have been years of social work involvement with the family, once proceedings are begun in the application for a care order, the statement in support should be 'focussing on the key significant historical events and concerns and rigorously avoiding all unnecessary detail' (Munby, 2013a:5).

How long should a chronology be? The President went on to say:

> We do not want social work chronologies extending over dozens of pages. Usually three or four at most will suffice. The background summary in the social work statement, particularly if it is cross-referenced to the chronology and avoids unnecessary repetition of what is already set out in the chronology, need be no more than a page or two.
>
> *Munby, 2013a:5*

The President has also made it clear that it is his intention to reduce the maximum size of the court bundle to 350 pages. Twenty years ago a typical file of case papers for the court hearing ('the bundle') tended to be much smaller. Whether the average increase in pages of evidence per case has improved court decision-making is highly debatable. The courts want the parties, in particular the local authority, to focus the attention of the court on that which is key.

The case's 'threshold statement' should be drafted in close consultation with the local authority lawyer. The process of doing so *before* the social work statement is finalized will help focus everyone's mind on what is really relevant. The President gave this fictional example in a 'typical' case of neglect to illustrate the level of detail that would be sufficient in a threshold statement:

> The parents have neglected the children. They have:
>
> - Not fed them properly.
> - Dressed them in torn and dirty clothes.

- Not supervised them properly.
- Not got them to school or to the doctor or hospital when needed.
- Not played with them or talked to them enough.
- Not listened to the advice of social workers, health visitors and others about how to make things better: and now will not let the social worker visit the children in the home [the evidence to support the case being identified by reference to the relevant page numbers in the bundle].

Munby, 2013a:5

Clearly, the key to good social work statements and threshold statements is to be *focused* and *succinct*.

The PLO tends to be revised and updated from time to time so it is essential that any child and family social worker and their lawyer is familiar with the most up-to-date version and produces application and documentation which comply with it.

As well as complying with the requirements of the PLO, it is essential that the social work statement reflects a thorough and fair approach by the social worker. The obligation to carry out the work to a high standard has been underlined by the courts. There can be no excuses, not least because the stakes are so high for the child and his or her parents.

The social worker's evidence and analysis must be of the highest standard; nothing less will do. The social worker's qualifications and experience are clearly relevant to the court. Although not specified in the PLO statement checklist, the social worker's first statement in the proceedings should always include a summary of their relevant qualifications and experience. There could also be a one-page curriculum vitae (CV) attached to the statement. It is not common for a judge to single out a social worker for criticism but it can happen. In the following case (see page 52) the High Court judge was critical of the local authority case handling and the social worker's casework and approach.

The quality of case work in the local authority office can have a very serious knock-on effect for the family and for the social worker. The court will scrutinize case handling (record-keeping, supervision, handovers etc.) and the individual approach of social workers to service users. Case handling and practice will be judged. Judges, particularly those being asked to sanction plans for adoption, will expect nothing less than thorough, principled, reasonable and respectful social work.

Re B-S (Children) [2013]

In *Re B-S (Children)* [2013], Sir James Munby, President of the Family Division, gave the judgment of the court. The issues raised and the guidance given in relation to social work evidence could not be more serious.

The judgment focused on local authority practice in cases where the local authority was seeking an adoption in the absence of parental consent. In those cases it was pointed out that the local authority asks the court to dispense with consent in accordance with s. 52(1)(b) Adoption and Children Act 2002, usually on the basis that the welfare of the child requires the consent to be dispensed with. However, there are also cases where the local authority asks for parental consent to be dispensed with because the parent lacks capacity. The judgment says that local authority evidence in support of adoption is not always adequate.

> We have real concerns, shared by other judges, about the recurrent inadequacy of the analysis and reasoning put forward in support of the case for adoption, both in the materials put before the court by local authorities and guardians and also in too many judgments. This is nothing new. But it is time to call a halt. [30]

The judgment highlights:

* there must be proper evidence both from the local authority and from the guardian;
* the central issue is what sort of placement best meets the child's needs;
* local authority and guardian evidence must address *all* the options which are realistically possible;
* it must contain an analysis of the arguments *for* and *against* each option (this might be, for example, comparing adoption to long-term fostering or placement with the extended family depending on the facts of the case);
* *negatives* as well as *positives* of the plan must be set out, including the risk of harm from each of the options;
* the narrative which sets out the recommendation must be *fully reasoned*, in other words it should be supported by the analysis of the pros and cons;
* the court will only make an adoption order if the evidence is clearly made out because adoption is a 'last resort'.

> **KEY CASE ANALYSIS**

Re IA (a Child) (Fact-finding; Welfare; Single Hearing; Experts Reports) [2013]

In this case, the case handling by the local authority was poor on account of no handover from the previous worker, which meant that assessment work wasn't as thorough as it should have been and consequently incorrect conclusions were reached.

The judge lamented that she 'should have been in the position of being able to place reliance upon the social work assessment so as to reach proper welfare determinations for IA' and 'should have had fair, balanced and proportionate advice resulting from a thorough inquiry undertaken over the five months or so since the proceedings were begun'. She should have 'been able to view the social workers as experts in relation to the child's welfare and to repose trust in their decision making'. This, however, was not the case because the social worker's work was 'of poor quality, superficial and, most worryingly of all, did not reflect the key principles which underpin the workings of the family justice system'.

Key principles cited by the judge that should be reflected in the social work statement are:

- 'children deserve an upbringing within their natural families';
- 'the local authority's duty should be to support and eventually reunite the family unless the risks are so high that the child's welfare requires alternative provision';
- 'Orders ratifying a care plan for adoption are "very extreme" only made when "necessary" for the protection of the children's interests, which means "when nothing else will do", "when all else fails".'

Key lessons for social workers providing evidence for care proceedings

Key lessons for social workers providing evidence for care proceedings include:

- local authority evidence must be *focused* on the relevant facts;
- the history should be as *succinct* as possible – there is no need to repeat what is detailed in other evidence already before the court;
- the evidence must address *all* the welfare *options* which are realistically possible and reflect core principles including that where possible children should be with their natural families;

- the evidence must contain an *analysis* of the arguments *for* and *against* each option (the positives and the negatives);
- the evidence must contain detail about the type of placement(s) that will best meet the children's needs;
- rigidly sticking to a checklist of factors and/or template pro forma and not going beyond it may result in an inadequate analysis of the options;
- difficulties in the working environment (poor handover/lack of support etc.) are no excuse for inadequate assessment and/or evidence;
- social workers must be and must be seen to be fair and respectful of the parents and must never 'put the boot in';
- a statement must distinguish clearly between what is fact and what is evaluation, assessment, analysis and opinion;
- a statement must distinguish between what is general background information and what is the specific evidence relied on to establish 'threshold' i.e. what is said to be causing significant harm or giving rise to a likelihood of significant harm to the child/children;
- social workers must carefully read and reflect upon the written evidence of the parents (paying particular attention to what the parents are saying) before giving evidence and being cross-examined.

It is not only in the area of children and families social work that you might be asked to provide a statement for a court. Whether it is for the Family Court or the Crown Court, a tribunal or a County Court, some general principles of good statement-writing practice apply. Your lawyer will help guide you as to the correct focus and will ensure that it is presented to the court in the correct format. It is also your responsibility to use:

- the court case/reference number on the front sheet;
- a header with the statement maker's name and whether or not it is their first/second etc. statement;
- large, clear typeface, sans serif;
- double line spacing;
- page numbers (page x of y in case pages get separated);
- short sentences;
- short paragraphs;
- plain English (no jargon);
- name, professional address, qualifications and registration details (if appropriate);
- technical terms used where appropriate and defined for the lay reader;
- numbered paragraphs and sections;

- headed sections;
- confidentiality warning in the header/footer if appropriate;

Finally, do not forget to sign and date the original copy. Until this is done it will not be acceptable to the court or the other parties.

Recommendations checklist

You can also check your own recommendations by asking yourself if they:

- reflect the principles of the relevant law;
- take into account all material facts including cultural and religious diversity;
- marshal the facts in a balanced way;
- where there is more than one set of competing facts, express recommendations in the alternative depending on which set of facts is found by the courts;
- indicate any literature, research or other material relied on;
- set out all the reasonable alternative options;
- summarize the range of opinion where there is a range of opinion on an issue in question;
- identify the advantages and disadvantages of each suggested course of action;
- analyse the alternative courses of action and weigh them up;
- reach a conclusion and show how it relates to the fact;
- indicate if the conclusion is provisional or qualified and, if so, the reasons for this and what further information is required;
- itemize any limitations – e.g. incomplete documentation;
- stay strictly within the author's area of expertise.

Further reading

Holt, K (2014) *Child Protection*: for more guidance on care proceedings see Kim Holt's book, also in the Focus on Social Work Law series.

Munby, J (2013a; 2013b; 2013c; 2013d; 2013e): the President of the Family Division and the Court of Protection (Sir James Munby) regularly sets out latest developments and proposed changes in 'View from the President's Chambers' – these can be found at www.judiciary.gov.uk/publications-and-reports/reports/family/view-from-presidents-chambers

4

BEING A WITNESS

AT A GLANCE THIS CHAPTER COVERS:

- what witnesses say about being a witness
- the process of giving evidence
- what courts and judges say
- what's really going on: cross-examination tactics and techniques
- witness preparation: doing it properly
- technology and virtual witness testimony

What witnesses say about being a witness

Consider the advice below from a professional witness who gave evidence in 2013. The witness had gone through witness preparation, including a mock cross-examination, and she knew her report inside out and back to front.

> The hardest thing is not to get defensive and emotional or start taking it personally when it is a sustained attack and no-one appears to be leaping to your aid – just accept this is par for the course and try to keep cool and professional – remember it's all just a game and the QC will be off butchering somebody else tomorrow.
>
> *Email correspondence from the witness to the author, 2013*

This witness's feedback chimes with the findings of a recent study in New Zealand (Henderson and Seymour, 2013). In that study expert witnesses were asked about their experiences in the criminal and family courts in New Zealand where the procedure during cross-examination is conducted in a very similar way to ours. Experts said they thought cross-examination felt like game-playing and attempts at trickery by the **advocate**. The researchers 'found strong support for the anecdotal reports that expert witnesses dislike the court process and would prefer to avoid any involvement'. However some positive news from this study was that many experts said that through 'experience or training they have learnt how to combat many cross-examination techniques'. (Henderson and Seymour, 2013:124)

What research and anecdotal reports from witnesses tell us is that giving evidence can be extremely daunting; a witness can feel very isolated in the witness box. Though the experience may be very unpleasant there are things that a witness can do to increase the chances that they will give their best evidence i.e. to give a complete, accurate and coherent account. Before looking at witness preparation techniques it is necessary to first understand what is going on in the courtroom when a witness gives evidence.

The process of giving evidence

The outcome of a case often turns on the judge's (or the jury's if one is present) evaluation of the evidence of the witnesses. Was it coherent? Was it accurate? Was it complete? Was it credible? In order to properly evaluate any witness's evidence, the trial judge must ensure that the witness is given the opportunity to tell their story in their own words and that the witness's evidence is properly tested. The witness's opportunity to tell their story in their own words is called **examination in chief** and the opportunity for an opposing party to test it is cross-examination.

The usual steps in the process are that the witness is called up to the witness box, they are invited to take an oath (swear on a holy book of the witness's choice) or to affirm (give a solemn promise) to tell the truth. After the witness chooses to swear or affirm the usher hands the appropriate card to the witness so that they can read the words from it (or they can the repeat the words as the usher says them bit by bit). From this point onwards the witness could be charged with the criminal offence of perjury unless they tell 'the truth, the whole truth and nothing but the truth'.

After the oath or affirmation the next step is called examination in chief. This is when the advocate calling the witness asks questions to enable the witness to explain. In a criminal case the witness will not usually have their written statement in front of them so they must give their evidence in chief from memory. In a civil case (including family cases) the witness's statement in writing is usually there in front of them (in a file or the bundle in the witness box) and the witness is asked to identify their statement and confirm if it is correct or not. Thus in a civil case a witness is not required to repeat the evidence that is written as everyone has had the chance to read it already. This is not the case in the criminal court where the judge or judge and jury are hearing the witness's evidence for the first time in examination in chief. After examination in chief comes cross-examination.

Cross-examination is when the opposing advocate challenges the witness by putting forward an alternative version of events. Cross-examination is usually done through leading questions, that is, questions which suggest or imply the desired answer. Cross-examination is as long or as short as piece of string; it depends on how many topics the cross-examiner wants to cover and in how much detail. Questions should always be relevant to the issues in the case but they need not be limited to what was written in the witness's statement or what they said in their evidence in chief. Advocates might have been required to give time estimates in advance stating how long they are likely to be when cross-examining the witness, but even when they do they do not always stick to them. In some cases the judge will take control in advance and impose maximum time limits on how long the advocate can be rather than leave it open-ended and completely in the hands of the advocate. This is more likely to happen if the witness is vulnerable on account of age or incapacity.

Finally, the witness may be re-examined by the advocate who called them up to the stand in the first place. **Re-examination** is for seeking clarification regarding things said under cross-examination. It is not a second bite at the examination-in-chief cherry; it is not a fresh chance for the advocate to invite the witness to tell parts of their story that didn't come out in examination in chief. That moment has already passed. Advocates will not always re-examine the witness because of its limited scope.

Judges sometimes ask questions during the witness's evidence. Some judges are more interventionist in this way than others. At the end of the witness's evidence (after re-examination, if any) the advocate who called the witness will usually ask the judge if they have any questions for the witness. If the judge does have any remaining questions he or she will ask them and then ask the advocates if there is anything they need to ask as a result.

At the very end of the witness's evidence the judge will signal to the witness that they may go, usually by saying 'Thank you, you may step down from the witness box now' or similar.

What courts and judges say

When facts are in dispute, in other words when there are different versions of events, the court needs to decide which one is true and courts like to see how the witness stands up to cross-examination.

Clarke v Edinburgh and District Tramways Co Ltd (1919) is a well-known House of Lords case which confirms the importance placed on observing the witness in order that the judge or the jury can evaluate their evidence. In that case Lord Shaw spoke of the advantages of seeing manner, hesitation, nuance of expression and 'even the turns of the eyelid'. In *Simmons v British Steel plc (Scotland)* [2004], also in the House of Lords, Lord Hope said: '[a]s everyone knows, the personality and demeanour of witnesses which printed words alone cannot capture plays a large part in an assessment of their credibility'. In other words courts like to observe witnesses under cross-examination before deciding whether or not to believe them. Issues can arise if the witness's face is not visible. One judge has said that Parliament should provide guidance for the courts; the issue in his case was whether to allow a defendant to wear a niqaab in court. He concluded in his case that she could but would need to remove it to give evidence.

> **KEY CASE ANALYSIS**

R v D(R) [2013]

On 16 September 2013, HHJ Peter Murphy gave a ruling in in relation to the wearing of a niqaab (a full face veil but with the eyes showing) by the defendant during proceedings in the Crown Court. The decision in *R v D(R)* attempts to balance the right to manifest a religious belief, the discomfort its removal might cause and the steps the court may be able to take to mitigate that discomfort against the principles of open justice and the requirements of a fair trial. The judge's conclusion was that in general 'the defendant is free to wear the niqaab during trial' but it would be:

> unfair to expect the juror to try to evaluate the evidence given by the person whom she cannot see, deprived of an essential tool for doing so: namely, being able to observe the demeanour of the witness; her reaction to being questioned; her reaction to other evidence as it is given.

The ruling in *R v D(R)* is not binding on other courts and until Parliament or a higher court (the Court of Appeal or the Supreme Court) sets down guidance it is uncertain how a court would respond to a request from a witness, including from a social worker, to give evidence in a niqaab. If the issue is raised with the court in advance it is hoped that suitable adjustments would be made. In *Re S (Practice: Muslim Women Giving Evidence)* [2007] the witness was a 21-year-old woman who was seeking to have her marriage annulled on the basis that she had been forced into it. She had concerns about removing her full face veil in order to give evidence but the court wanted to see her face to assess whether she was telling the truth or not. The judge was female but one of the lawyers was male. The hearing went ahead with the witness removing her face veil because the entrance into the court was monitored to ensure that any man entering would be stopped and the male lawyer was screened from seeing the witness without her face veil by means of 'a large umbrella'.

It is normal to feel anxious about the prospect of giving evidence. In 1949 Lord Denning, one of the most famous English judges ever, wrote: 'When cross-examination is properly conducted, it is not only <u>not</u> unfair to the witness, but it is a most valuable instrument in ascertaining the truth.' Alex McBride said in his book about life as a criminal barrister (2011) that barristers agree that: '[Cross-examination] is beyond doubt the greatest legal engine ever invented for the discovery of the truth.'

Cross-examination is when the court can evaluate how the witness responds when their evidence is challenged. Does the witness remain certain? Does he change his mind? Does she say that she can no longer remember that well? Does he get defensive? No judge expects a witness to have a perfect memory of events that took place a long time ago, in fact they might think it suspicious if a witness claimed a perfect memory.

In *Ultraframe (UK) Ltd v Fielding* (2005) the judge noted that witnesses were:

> being asked to remember events that had taken place up to seven years previously. It did not surprise me that some of the witnesses had only vague recollections of meetings, and some had no real grasp of dates. [20]

A judge might not look so kindly upon a social worker who in their professional role should be making records of relevant events. When faced with the prospect of giving evidence a social worker must prepare thoroughly for court. Preparation starts with a thorough review of the case notes and making the statement using those records. Uncertainty about service user details or vagueness about what happened when might mean the judge or jury decides not to place any or much weight on what you say.

Scientists are beginning to challenge the theory that cross-examination is a great tool for getting to the truth. In the book *Witness Testimony: Psychological, Investigative and Evidential Perspectives* (2006), Professor Elizabeth Loftus says that '[o]ur accumulating body of scientifically-based knowledge [of the hidden influences that interfere with mental processes and memory] has scotched the old-time assumption that all would be revealed in the witness box' and she calls examination and cross-examination 'impoverished' tools. As yet scientific theories have not made

---

PRACTICE FOCUS

Cross-examination – example 1 (a professional witness in a civil case)

Q: So in fact you did send material in addition to the letter we have seen. That's right isn't it?
A: I would have to go back and look through the files to confirm that. It sounds like it from the letter doesn't it?
Q: It also sounds from your answer that you weren't engaged in the process; is that right?
A: No, but if they had asked me to send something and I had sent it, that doesn't mean I would remember now.
Q: There is no reason to doubt the letter is there?
A: No. Yes, that's fine.

Cross-examination – example 2 (a four-year-old witness, the victim of a sexual assault, in a criminal case)

Q: Was it something you made up? Who's idea was it then?
A: No one's
Q: Did you think it up yourself?
A: [Witness shakes head]
Q: We have to have an answer from you, you see ... I have to wait until I get your answer because I cannot ask you any more questions ... Are you going to answer that question for me?

Cross-examination – example 3 (a professional witness in a disciplinary hearing)

Q: Presumption is pretty bad, speculation on your part is just as bad, is it not?
A: I agree we ought not to speculate but we have clearly set out that it's a presumption and not a factual remark.
Q: I will end the day on this note. You see what this presumption does, I suggest, reveal your entire mindset which is to lean in favour of the executive counsel's case in your theory, in your mindset. Do you agree with that?
A: That's not my own view.

These three extracts are from actual cross-examination by three eminent QCs. Read each one again. Which of the three rules of cross-examination (opposite) are being applied?

significant changes to the way things have been done in the courtroom for hundreds of years. If your evidence is challenged, expect to be cross-examined. Prepare, prepare, prepare.

What's really going on: cross-examination tactics and techniques

Advocates are taught that cross-examination is their opportunity to challenge the witness and that the best way to do that to robust adults is to follow some simple rules. These are:

1 *Use leading questions* – ask questions that suggest the answer because the witness is more likely to agree with you. In other words, when you cross-examine you tell the witness – you don't ask.
2 *Control the witness* – Ultimate control is knowing the answer to the question before you ask it. Fishing expeditions are dangerous.
3 *Tell don't ask* – never let the witness explain.

Did you identify the following cross-examination techniques in the Practice Focus box opposite?

Example 1: this shows the advocate leading the witness by making a statement and then tagging on to the end of the statement 'That's right isn't it?'. This is a common technique as is making a statement and adding on 'is it not?' A social worker might be asked 'Best practice in those circumstances is to obtain specialist advice, is it not?' or 'You went to the house three times that month and you never managed to see the child once, that's right isn't it?'

Example 2: In this example the cross-examiner is trying to stay in control of the child witness: 'We have to have an answer from you, you see … I have to wait until I get your answer because I cannot ask you any more questions'. A similar approach might be taken with you if you give evidence.

Example 3: This shows a cross-examiner trying to tell the professional witness that she was biased. The advocate is telling the witness and asking her to agree with it. The witness is being led and is not being asked to explain. The cross-examiner is trying to take control by in effect making a mini-speech to the tribunal. You might be told: 'You did not follow best practice did you?' 'You failed to follow the guidance in *Working Together* – you didn't did you?'

Witness preparation: doing it properly

Boston attorney and former Harvard Law School lecturer Dan Small says the purpose of witness preparation is:

> (1) to level the playing field and (2) to allow the witness to take control ... despite all appearances of the questioner being in control, the whole point of the exercise is to get the witness's testimony. Because of this, the witness has a right to take control, not in an adversarial way, but in a very simple way by following [witness preparation's] basic rules.
>
> *Small, 2009*

Can preparation help the social worker deal with cross-examination techniques? Research says it can. In 'laboratory research', that is simulated courtroom cross-examination exercises, Wheatcroft and Ellison (2012) found that witness preparation is a worthwhile endeavour because it can increase confidence and thus positively affect the witness's demeanour.

One of the key parts of **witness familiarization** is getting used to going to court first as an observer. Most court cases are open to the public save for family cases. Go along to any Crown Court and watch a trial from the public gallery – you must get permission from the judge if you want to take notes. To observe a Family Court case, ask a colleague if you can shadow them and the lawyer will ask the judge permission for you to sit in.

When you know you are going to give evidence as part of your social work role, get as much support as possible from the lawyers who are calling you as a witness. Your lawyers might be able to recommend a witness preparation course. They should certainly advise you on practical matters such as what the courtroom will look like, who the judge is likely to be, what to wear, what to take with you etc. When you meet with your lawyers ask them about the process, no question is too simple.

Box 4.1: Suggested questions to ask your lawyer

1 What time should I arrive at court?
2 Can I go to the court and see the actual courtroom first to get familiar with it?
3 Where should I meet you/where should I wait?
4 Will I sit or do I stand in the witness box?
5 Will I be able to see and refer to my statement/report?

6 How long am I likely to be in the witness box?
7 What time will it start/finish?
8 What is the dress code?
9 What do I call the judge?
10 Do I need to bring anything with me e.g. cases files, copies of my report etc.?

Ask your lawyer practical questions about the process in your particular case. Getting the answers will help reduce any anxiety and allow you to concentrate on preparing to give evidence rather than being bamboozled by unfamiliar surroundings or alien procedures.

Your lawyer must not tell you what to say in your evidence (that would be 'coaching') but they can and should tell you about the procedures of the courtroom. The Court of Appeal, in *R v Momodou and Limani* (2005), made it clear that coaching must not occur but 'sensible preparation for the experience of giving evidence, which assists the witness to give of his or her best at the forthcoming trial, is permissible'.

A 'dry run' or 'dress-rehearsal' of the witness's evidence for a forthcoming case is definitely not allowed but mock cross-examination on a fictional case study is an excellent way to feel more confident about your courtroom skills. Many social workers undergo this as part of professional development training. It is highly recommended that you do too if you haven't already. Witness preparation is a good thing for the witness but only if it is done properly.

'Purdah' is a term that you might not be familiar with but is a very important aspect of giving evidence. A witness is 'in purdah' when giving evidence which means they should not speak to anyone about their evidence when they are on a break, for example, over lunch or overnight if their evidence stretches beyond more than one court day. If you need to speak to your lawyers about something, during the lunch break, for example, the judge would need to give special permission. The 'purdah' rule exists to avoid the possibility that a witness could be improperly influenced or 'assisted' during a break but while they are still in the midst of giving evidence. Of course, when you have finished giving evidence and the judge says something like 'Thank you, you may step down' you are no longer in purdah and can speak to others about the case as long as they are not prospective witnesses in the case.

Since you will be in purdah whilst giving evidence, ask your lawyer all your queries and raise your concerns *before* you start your evidence.

Once you are in the witness box there are some simple strategies you can adopt to help you give you best evidence.

Box 4.2: Ten top tips for the witness box

1 Know your statement/report and (if you have a copy) refer to it.
2 Look at the questioner when they are speaking to you.
3 Listen to the question, take your time and think about the answer.
4 Turn your head and look at the decision-maker(s) when you give your evidence.
5 Slow down (most witnesses are nervous and as a result tend to speak too fast).
6 Stop when you have finished your answer, don't fill pregnant pauses.
7 Tell the truth, but if you don't understand the question say so; if you don't know say so; don't guess or speculate.
8 If necessary, ask the judge 'May I explain?' She is most likely to want you to.
9 If you make an honest mistake – correct/clarify as soon as possible.
10 Remember purdah when you are on a break.

On-the-spot question On the basis of what you have read, how might you overcome any worries or anxieties you might have about giving evidence in court?

Technology and virtual attendance at court

Although TV links to witnesses within the court building are often used for those who are intimidated or vulnerable due to age or incapacity, generally very little use is made of technology to allow witness evidence away from the court. Think how much travel time it could save the social worker and others if they could be linked into a court hearing by video? Video links have been used in the past to take the evidence from a witness in a nursing home or a hospital or in another country. But these are the exceptions rather than the rule. Couldn't Skype be used more often?

In *Re ML (Use of Skype Technology)* [2013], Jackson J said that Skype:

can be very effective for informal use, but does not lend itself to the court environment. There are problems in everyone seeing and hearing the picture and in the evidence being recorded. There are also issues about security. I would not be willing to use this method if there was any alternative.

Re ML (Use of Skype Technology) *[2013] [11]*

In 2013 the new Lord Chief Justice used his very first press conference to say that video-call technology such as Skype and FaceTime could be used to allow criminal defendants to take part in pre-trial hearings without coming to court. There is a lot of scope for greater use of technology in courts to patch people in from elsewhere, but it is early days.

Box 4.3: Essential reminders for witnesses

Do

- Tell your lawyer if you spot errors or omissions in any of the papers.
- Arrive at court in good time.
- Make sure you know whom to meet, where and when.
- Make sure you know what to bring (e.g. any case files – your lawyer can advise you).
- Dress smartly, showing respect for the court.
- Take along food/snack (it may be a long wait) but remember not to eat or drink in court.
- Refer to the barristers as 'counsel' not 'Mr X' or 'Ms Y'.
- Look at the judge/jury when you are speaking.
- Look at the barrister when he/she is speaking.
- Stand up if you wish to feel more in control (but note in some hearings you will be expected to sit e.g. the family proceedings court).
- Project your voice.
- Talk slowly enough for the judge to take notes.
- Be ready to 'watch the judge's pen'.
- Use the bundle (including your statement) in the witness box if it helps.
- Answer the questions – you are not there to evade them!
- Turn off your mobile phone *before* you enter the courtroom.
- Be ready to explain to the court important parts of your experience that entitle you to call yourself 'expert'.

- Think about jargon/technical terms that may need to be explained to the judge.

Don't

- Use long sentences.
- Use jargon.
- Wear anything uncomfortable or garish.
- Eat or drink in court (save for water supplied by the court).
- Chew gum.
- Talk at the same time as the judge/counsel.
- Talk to anyone involved in the case whilst you are on 'a break' (purdah) from your evidence.
- Feel you have to answer 'yes/no' if the answer is not that straightforward.
- Struggle on if you need a break for the toilet/feel ill.
- Argue or try to score points with counsel.
- Produce last-minute material in the witness box, unless already shown to your lawyer and they have discussed it with the other parties.

Remember: the way you give evidence affects the weight attached to it. You are there to assist the decision-maker and, above all, to tell the truth.

Further reading

Henderson, E and F Seymour (2013) *Expert Witnesses under Examination in the New Zealand Criminal and Family Courts*: in this study the experiences of expert witnesses reveal just how challenging cross-examination can be and how they deal with it.

Loftus, E (2013) 'Elizabeth Loftus: The fiction of memory' on TED talks www.ted.com/talks/elizabeth_loftus_the_fiction_of_memory.html: this talk challenges the traditional assumptions about testimony that relies on witness memory.

McBride, A (2011) *Defending the Guilty: Truth and Lies in the Criminal Courtroom*: this book is an eye-opener for non-lawyers who want to understand what goes on between advocates and their clients in criminal cases.

5

WORKING WITH OTHER PROFESSIONALS IN THE LEGAL SYSTEM

AT A GLANCE THIS CHAPTER COVERS:

- working together
- local authority lawyers
- the police
- the CPS
- intermediaries
- solicitors
- barristers
- guardians
- expert witnesses
- independent social workers
- litigants in person, McKenzie friends and more

Working together

A social worker might find herself consulting local authority lawyers for advice about how to protect a child, she might provide a statement to solicitors for a vulnerable adult for the Court of Protection or a statement to the police as a witness to a criminal matter. She might also work alongside an intermediary in a police interview. Situations like this require understanding of those other professional roles in order to achieve the best working relationships. The chapter contains examples of good practice as well as barriers to effective working based on actual cases.

This chapter does not seek to replicate *Working Together to Safeguard Children* (DfE, 2013b) guidance which explains how organizations should work together to safeguard children and how practitioners should conduct assessments of children. *Working Together* is a document that every social worker should be familiar with. It emphasizes the need for organizations to take a coordinated approach and the legal responsibilities of:

- schools and colleges;
- early years and childcare;
- health services;
- the police;
- adult social care services;
- housing authorities;
- the British Transport Police;
- the prison service;
- the probation service;
- the secure estate for children (this includes secure training centres and young offender institutions);
- the UK Border Agency;
- the Children and Family Court Advisory and Support Service (Cafcass);
- the armed services;
- the voluntary and private sectors; and
- faith organizations.

When working with, or attempting to work with, one of the above organizations to promote the welfare of a child or protect them from harm, the *Working Together* 2013 guidance should be the social worker's first reference point in respect of children.

Similarly, when working to safeguard vulnerable adults, social workers will need to work with housing, health, the police and other agencies. Safeguarding adults also requires working collaboratively rather than duplicating existing work or over-stepping professional boundaries.

Local authority lawyers

The person a social worker is most likely to come to rely on in legal proceedings is their own 'in-house' lawyer. Local authority lawyers (who may be qualified solicitors or barristers – see below) are also often known as in-house lawyers because they work for the local authority within its legal team. Some local authorities have tendered out the service to law firms. The lawyers are on call, literally, for social workers to consult but there will sometimes be a 'gatekeeper' who determines whether or not it is a suitable query for the legal team. Normally, if a social worker wants to consult the legal team for advice they would need to go through their manager first unless it is an emergency.

Once it is agreed that you can get legal advice, you might have to complete paperwork setting out in broad terms what you need advice about and then there will be a planning discussion with the lawyer either face to face or on the telephone. Your lawyer can advise on the law but only once you have given them the facts and you must have these at your fingertips. Bear in mind that, just like social workers, some will be more experienced than others or your query might be particularly complex so they might have to go away and research the answer before they get back to you.

You are wasting your time and the lawyer's if you have this discussion unprepared. Imagine you are seeking advice on whether or not there are grounds to remove a child under an emergency protection order but you fail to pass on the details of the most recent case conference. Mistakes can and do occur. In *Re X (Emergency Protection Orders)* [2006], a number of errors had been made in that case by both social workers and their legal advisor though there was 'no evidence of any malevolent or unpro-fessional motive'. The judge firmly set down detailed guidelines to assist in future cases where an emergency protection order for a child is contemplated and sought.

If you miss out a valuable piece of information or give the incorrect information, the consequences could be devastating: a child could be removed when they should not have been, or vice versa; your working relationship with the family could be permanently damaged or worse destroyed; and the lawyer's and the local authority's reputations may be harmed.

The stakes are high when court orders give the state power to intervene in people's personal lives; there is a heavy onus on social workers to furnish their lawyers with full and accurate information. Advice based on incorrect or incomplete information is shaky at best.

Once engaged in court proceedings, the case will take on a timetable all of its own. Judges set dates by which material must be disclosed, or exchanged between the parties. Hearing and meeting dates become fixed by the court and, if the material is not produced in accordance with the timetable, the hearings or meetings may be ineffective. Time and money may be wasted. Costs may be ordered against a party, in some rare cases even against an individual. If your lawyer gives you a deadline, unless you are told otherwise, assume it is necessary to meet a court requirement. If you foresee that you will not be able to meet that deadline, notify the lawyer immediately; they may be able to negotiate an extension, but don't count on it.

Don't allow cases to drift along; if there comes a time when you think you need legal advice, get it. You might well need to discuss this with your manager in the first place but listen to your instincts. The more notice the legal department has the better because planned applications are preferable to short notice, emergency ones. Of course, there will be cases where emergencies arise. You should also be able to obtain out-of-hours advice. Lord Laming said, in the report into the death of Victoria Climbié:

> No emergency action on a case concerning an allegation of
> deliberate harm to a child should be taken without first
> obtaining legal advice. Local authorities must ensure that
> such legal advice is available 24 hours a day. (Laming, 2003:
> para. 5.128)

Legal advice need not be followed. It is only advice in the sense that the decision is the client's (the client being the social work department), but it should not be gone against lightly and certainly not without approval at team-manager level or above.

Box 5.1: The three most important things you can do for your local authority lawyer

1 Be clear about what it is you want to achieve in practical terms e.g. access to your service user to undertake an assessment, stopping someone harassing the reception staff, stopping a newspaper publication about a vulnerable service user etc.
2 Set out the facts logically, fairly, without embellishment and based on reliable records.
3 Meet deadlines – particularly those that have been set by the court.

The police

It is rather obvious to say it, but the police's role is to ensure that laws are not broken and to work to keep a peaceful and safe society. Part of that role involves detecting and investigating crimes. The police rely on social workers sharing information with them when appropriate (see also Chapter 2). Social workers must work closely with the police and share information about crimes or suspected crimes. Reviews of practice after the terrible murders of Holly Wells and Jessica Chapman underlined why.

Box 5.2: The 'Soham murders'

In 2002 Holly Wells and Jessica Chapman were murdered in Soham, Cambridgeshire, by the school caretaker Ian Huntley. Previously, Huntley had had a series of relationships or sexual encounters with a number of young women while he was living in North East Lincolnshire in the 1990s. Opportunities were missed by agencies to share information with the police that would have added to the intelligence about Huntley as a systematic offender. The case illustrates that the police rely on intelligence from social workers about individuals who have committed crimes or are suspected of having committed crimes; sharing information can help police identify a pattern of behaviour. As Sir Christopher Kelly said, in the serious case review of this case:

> There were significant shortcomings and inconsistencies in the way information was shared between some of the agencies, particularly social services and the police; and some of

> the connections which could have been made to identify a
> pattern in Ian Huntley's behaviour were missed. (Kelly, 2004:
> para. 229)

If police have gathered the evidence about a suspected crime, they will pass on the evidence to the CPS (see below) which will consider whether or not to prosecute. Whilst the police do not themselves make the decisions about whether or not to prosecute, police officers carrying out investigations and gathering evidence will have in mind how the evidence might play out at trial, if it goes that far.

Effective collaboration is essential when the police investigate a possible crime against a vulnerable adult or child. Be clear about your role within the police investigation and beware of conflicts that might arise: are you part of the investigative team? If so then you are not impartial and should not also take on the role of supporting a service user or a member of the service user's family. Are you a supporter? If so, then you cannot be an impartial investigator. The supporter would be responsible for welfare issues and would not take part in the *Achieving Best Evidence* (ABE) interview (see MoJ, 2011a; and Chapter 6 below). A supporter could help the interviewers plan the ABE interview (advising on how best to conduct it from the witness's welfare perspective) and they could observe but could not participate as an interviewer. Are you facilitating communication? If you are taking on a role akin to an intermediary (see Chapter 6), then you cannot also be a witness supporter. As a facilitator of communication you must be impartial and assist without influencing the question or answer. Your role must be transparent and neutral. You cannot be more than one of these roles (investigator, witness supporter, communication facilitator) at the same time. They are mutually incompatible. It is important to be clear from the outset what your role is.

If the local authority has a care order for the child who is a potential witness, and the child does not have capacity to consent, their social worker should be asked, for example, for permission to interview the child or for them to undergo a medical examination. In the case of a vulnerable adult who does not have capacity to consent to an interview, a social worker's views may be sought as to whether it is in their best interests to be interviewed or medically examined. Interviews and medical examinations must not be conducted without consent from the witness or, if they do not have capacity to consent, then there has to have been a decision that it is in his or her best interests. Issues of capacity, consent and autonomy are outside the scope of this book, however, readers will find Robert Johns' (2014) book in this series, *Capacity and Autonomy*, extremely helpful.

The police may conduct what is known as an ABE interview (and *Achieving Best Evidence in Criminal Proceedings* (MoJ, 2011a) is also covered in the Chapter 6). Police officers are specially trained in how to conduct interviews in accordance with the guidance. Some social workers are also specially trained to conduct ABE interviews but should only do so if it is agreed as the most appropriate way forward in the police investigation. The decision on who leads will depend on who is able to establish the best rapport with the witness. The police still maintain overall responsibility for the conduct of the investigation, therefore the planning of the interview must be done together and the social worker must feel confident that they understand the evidential requirements, i.e. what needs to be covered in the interview in terms of the elements of the offence being investigated.

If you attend an ABE interview, be clear about your role. Police officers might erroneously refer to you as an 'appropriate adult'. You are not. The role of the appropriate adult applies to a police suspect (and is dealt with in Chapter 6). You may be asked to be a witness supporter and if so you will want to consider whether it is best for the witness if you are in the interview suite or outside it, perhaps observing and listening in. Being involved in the ABE interview does not necessarily mean sitting in on the interview. If there is already an intermediary assisting the witness and police officer to communicate with each other, a social worker present would result in three adults in the room which may not be in the witness's interests. If this is likely to be the case, discuss the situation with the interviewing officer and the intermediary. You may decide that it is better if you observe from the control room.

Apart from investigating crimes, police and social workers often work closely together on safeguarding issues. For example, it may be necessary for a police officer to use his powers to ensure the immediate protection of a child.

> The police have emergency powers under section 46 of the Children Act 1989 to enter premises and remove a child to ensure their immediate protection. This power can be used if the police have reasonable cause to believe a child is suffering or is likely to suffer significant harm. Police emergency powers can help in emergency situations but should be used

only when necessary. Wherever possible, the decision to remove a child from a parent or carer should be made by a court.

Working Together to Safeguard Children, DfE, 2013b:52

If the police do use their powers under s. 46 Children Act 1989, they must inform child protection social workers and agree on the next steps. What is the plan for the child? Have the parents been informed? Who should have contact with the child? The police power only lasts for a maximum of 72 hours (s. 46(6)) and does not confer parental responsibility on the police. The social workers will need to identify whether or not the local authority wishes to obtain a court order in order for the local authority to share parental responsibility.

Police also have a role in safeguarding adults, for example, under mental health legislation they may take a person to a place of safety for up to 72 hours if they find someone in a public place who appears to be 'suffering from mental disorder and to be in immediate need of care or control' (s. 136 Mental Health Act 1983).

Relationships between the police and social care can sometimes be strained. This can be on account of a number of factors, including neither wishing to share too much information (the police officer because she does not wish to reveal too much about an ongoing investigation and the social worker because he is being protective of his service user and their personal information). This, of course, has an impact on the way in which people work together.

> ◤ **PRACTICE FOCUS**
>
> A teenage child who is the subject of a care order alleges she has been assaulted by her father following a dispute in a public place. A joint investigation is considered at a strategy meeting between the police and social care. Police want the girl to be medically examined. Social workers, following a case conference, disagree with the police on the basis that it isn't in the child's interests. The disagreement is escalated to senior level – Head of Child Abuse Command and Head of Children's Services.
>
> - If the matter is not agreed, can the court be asked to make a ruling as to whether the child should be medically examined or not?

The CPS

The CPS decision whether or not to prosecute is a serious one affecting the accused, the victims, witnesses and others. After it came to light that there had been numerous, never prosecuted allegations against Jimmy Savile, the CPS reviewed how it had made its decisions. Updated guidance was issued. How those decisions are taken is now governed by the *Code for Crown Prosecutors* (2013a): 'The Code gives guidance to prosecutors on the general principles to be applied when making decisions about prosecutions.' (para. 1.3) It sets out the two-stage test: (i) the evidential stage; followed by (ii) the public interest stage.

Prosecutors must be satisfied that there is sufficient evidence to provide a realistic prospect of conviction against each suspect on each charge. They must consider what the defence case may be, and how it is likely to affect the prospects of conviction. A case which does not pass the evidential stage must not proceed, no matter how serious or sensitive it may be.

… In every case where there is sufficient evidence to justify a prosecution, prosecutors must go on to consider whether a prosecution is required in the public interest.

It has never been the rule that a prosecution will automatically take place once the evidential stage is met. A prosecution will usually take place unless the prosecutor is satisfied that there are public interest factors tending against prosecution which outweigh those tending in favour. In some cases the prosecutor may be satisfied that the public interest can be properly served by offering the offender the opportunity to have the matter dealt with by an out-of-court disposal rather than bringing a prosecution.

Code for Crown Prosecutors, 2013: paras 4.4, 4.7, 4.8

Remember that even though the local authority might have enough evidence to proceed and succeed with an application for a care order, the CPS might not be in a position to proceed. In a criminal case the allegations must be proved 'beyond reasonable doubt' whereas in a Family Court the civil standard applied is 'the balance of probability'. In other words the evidence for a criminal case must reach a higher standard for the case to be successful.

Decisions whether or not to prosecute are of vital importance to victims as this quote from a victim of child sexual exploitation, Girl A, shows:

> Detectives from Operation Span made the strongest case they could to the CPS and then waited for them to react ... They dug their heels in for a while, until Mr Afzal looked at the case afresh and decided it was time to bite the bullet. It was one of his first decisions in the job as chief prosecutor and I think he realised that by taking it he was giving me – and all the girls like me – a voice. I'll always be grateful to him for that.
>
> *Girl A and Bunyan, 2013: 282*

Perhaps you are supporting a service user who has complained of being a victim of a criminal offence. If you are not satisfied with the CPS's decision in a case, ask for the reasons. If your service user is the victim, they have rights under the *Code of Practice for Victims of Crime* (MoJ, 2013a). They are entitled to be informed about how they can 'seek a review of CPS decisions not to prosecute, to discontinue or offer no evidence in all proceedings; and can ask for the decision to be reviewed'. Discontinuing a case after it has started or offering no evidence once the matter is at court are two other ways in which the CPS might not proceed with (or 'drop') a case.

Social workers who provide witness statements as part of their job to the police in a case that is prosecuted by the CPS will usually find that their in-house lawyers act as their liaison with the CPS. This is also true in cases where the social worker seeks information from the CPS; for instance, the CPS might decide not to prosecute a carer for the alleged assault on a child and the DVD of the child's ABE interview might be valuable evidence in the care proceedings. Ensure that your legal advisors are aware of any involvement you have with the police or the CPS.

If there are linked family and criminal cases running at the same time a Protocol and Good Practice Model which came into force at the start of 2014 must now be followed (CPS, 2013b). It was issued jointly by the President of the Family Division, the Senior Presiding Judge in the criminal courts and the Director of Public Prosecutions (DPP) on behalf of the CPS. It is particularly important to address issues concerning disclosure of Family Court evidence in the criminal case and vice versa. The lack of joined-up thinking or joined-up action between the two sets of proceedings can be lamentable; this can lead to delay and may be contrary to the welfare of the child. *A Local Authority v DG and Others* [2014] illustrates that the Family Courts are becoming less tolerant of poor cooperation. Be ready to assist your lawyers when they require information and records from you to disclose to the CPS.

Intermediaries

Intermediaries are also covered in some detail in Chapter 6. A good definition appears in *Achieving Best Evidence* (MoJ, 2011a):

> **Intermediary**: one of the Special Measures which the Youth Justice and Criminal Evidence Act 1999 (Section 29) allows for certain eligible witnesses is that they may give evidence (both examination-in-chief and cross-examination) through an intermediary. An intermediary must be approved by the court, and assists by communicating to the witness the questions which are put to them, and to anyone asking such questions the answer given by the witness in reply to them. The intermediary may explain the questions or answers to the extent necessary to enable them to be understood. An intermediary may also be called on to assist in the making of a video-recording with a view to making it the witness's evidence-in-chief. In such a case the court will decide whether it was appropriate to use the intermediary when deciding whether to admit the recording in evidence. Only witnesses eligible on grounds of age or incapacity may receive the assistance of an intermediary under the Act, although the court also has inherent powers to call on an intermediary in other cases. The 1999 Act does not deal with the court's powers to call on the assistance of signed or spoken language interpreters, but it recognises that all courts have such powers.
>
> *MoJ, 2011a:152–53*

Intermediaries can be the key to unlocking cases involving offences against vulnerable people that previously might have been thought of as too difficult to investigate or take to court. Some witnesses can be thought of as simply 'too difficult to interview'. You could find that your service user, on account of their age or incapacity, might not even get to give an initial interview, let alone a recorded ABE interview passed to the CPS for a charging decision. If you or colleagues know a registered intermediary (RI) who works with vulnerable witnesses, you could ask them to come in to give a talk about their role. Their impact can be remarkable as this next case shows.

> **KEY CASE ANALYSIS**

R v IA and Others [2013]

This case involved the trial of a husband, wife and their daughter for what amounted to a nine-year exploitation of a deaf young woman trafficked by them from Pakistan. RB, the victim in the case, was brought to England in 2000 when she was perhaps 12 years old. She was profoundly deaf, without speech and unable to read or write. The Home Office allowed her entry as a domestic worker in a private household. She was a servant in the household, living in the basement, working without pay, being loaned out to other members of the family and to do menial chores for the son's business. As a later jury found, she was also raped on numerous occasions by Mr A. After being given indefinite leave to remain in this country, the defendants opened a bank account in her name and helped her to fill out forms so that false claims could be made for over £30,000 of income support, housing benefit (there was a sham tenancy agreement) and council tax benefits.

In 2009 the authorities came across RB. First, they wanted to establish whether any offences had been committed against RB; they sought the assistance of a deaf intermediary from a very early stage for what may be one of the most intensive and lengthy involvements of an intermediary in any case. Some language had to be devised in which she could communicate. RB and the intermediary developed an idiosyncratic sign language during a series of rapport-building meetings. There followed 14 video-recorded ABE interviews, which were played to the jury at the trial and she was cross-examined at length. RB's evidence was only made possible by the help of the intermediary.

As the next chapter also describes, intermediaries are also a vital resource for vulnerable defendants. Without intermediaries many vulnerable defendants would simply not be able to participate effectively in their trials.

Solicitors in law firms

Solicitors usually carry out the bulk of day-to-day legal work, apart from advocacy in court. They give pre-proceedings advice and handle pre-trial preparation. Solicitors can, however, appear as advocates in the magistrates' hearing and they can appear in the Crown Court and higher courts (High Court, Court of Appeal and Supreme Court) if they have qualified for the right of audience there.

Solicitors representing parents can and very often do appear as advocates in family proceedings. A party seeking legal advice, such as a parent who has been told that the local authority is contemplating applying for a care order, or a defendant arrested on suspicion of committing a crime, will usually first approach a solicitor in a law firm for legal advice. Whether or not they receive publicly funded advice and representation depends on the legal aid rules. Public spending cutbacks have severely limited the amount of money available for legal aid. Currently, parents who are **respondents** in care proceedings are still guaranteed public funding for their lawyers.

The Law Society represents solicitors and runs the Children Law Accreditation Scheme. Members of the Law Society's Children Law Accreditation Scheme, when representing a party in proceedings covered by the Children Act 1989, agree to be bound by a special code of practice. Practitioners who are not scheme members can also undertake children law work but will not be identified as specialists. Parents will sometimes ask social workers to recommend a local solicitor and some offices will keep lists of local specialists or will direct the parent to the Citizen's Advice Bureau which will usually keep such a list.

Junior solicitors tend to be known as 'associates'. A solicitor who is an owner of the law firm is known as 'partner' and the person who runs the firm is known as the 'senior partner'.

Barristers

Barristers are first and foremost advocates and spend the majority of their working lives being advocates in court. There are over 15,000 barristers, mostly in self-employed practice. Many qualified barristers are employed by companies, the Government Legal Service or the CPS and are known as the 'employed' Bar. Most of the advocates in the Crown Court are barristers; however, a substantial number of prosecution advocates are now CPS 'crown advocates' and many defence advocates are defence solicitors who have qualified to be 'higher court advocates' or 'solicitor advocates'.

Self-employed barristers practise from 'chambers', which is an association of barristers who share the overheads and costs of premises and of employing staff, in particular the clerk who is the business manager. Because they are all self-employed it is possible for one member of chambers to appear in the same case as another member of chambers.

Perhaps one of the biggest surprises that can occur is that the barrister in a case can change at the last minute. This occurs because barristers who are booked in advance may find that a previous case overruns and therefore they are no longer free. Their clerks will then pass on the brief (usually to another member of the same chambers) who may have to get to grips with a large amount of reading material at very short notice. Barristers are used to doing this.

Once at court you will want to meet with your barrister. Barristers call this 'having a conference' with their client. It is important to arrive early enough for this to happen before the court calls the case in. A social worker should not enter into discussions involving the representative of the other party unless and until their own barrister is there. Because of the limited resources, most barristers at court have no administrative assistance. They are running the show for the local authority and need your assistance; make sure that you arrive in good time, with sufficient copies of the necessary, completed paperwork.

> I had a case where I was running around the court house amending and photocopying statements an hour before the hearing. It left me with insufficient time to have full and proper conference with the social worker or negotiations with the other parties, and I left the court feeling aggrieved. Situations like this can make it a lot harder to persuade the court that the care plan will be competently executed!
>
> *Email from the barrister to the author, 2013*

Experienced barristers can apply to 'take silk'. If their application is successful they are appointed Queen's Counsel and are entitled to use the letters QC after their name. They are known as 'leading counsel' and those who are not silks are 'juniors'. Only a small proportion of practising barristers will make it to the rank of silk. Serious and complex cases will require a silk and a junior so that the client has two barristers working on the case. When there is a silk and a junior the silk usually conducts the lion's share of the advocacy in court, including delivering the opening and closing speeches on behalf of the client they represent.

Cafcass guardians

Cafcass stands for the Children and Family Court Advisory and Support Service. It was set up on 1 April 2001 and brought together the family court services previously provided by the Family Court Welfare Service, the Guardian ad Litem Service and the Children's Division of the Official Solicitor's Office. Representatives of Cafcass are appointed to help over 145,000 children every year in court proceedings (care, adoption and private law proceedings) in order to put forward an independent view regarding the child's best interests. Cafcass is also there to ensure that through the representative the child has a voice in the proceedings.

It is important to assist the Cafcass officer by inviting them to all formal planning meetings you have in respect of the child/children (including statutory reviews, case conferences and adoption panels), responding promptly to their emails/telephone calls and giving them access to your files. This is not simply a matter of good practice; the Cafcass representative is entitled under the Children Act 1989 to access local authority records which are relevant to the case in question.

Difficulties working with a Cafcass officer will hopefully be rare though the stresses on the Cafcass system are well documented. In 2012, senior barrister Martha Cover wrote about the negative impact of severe delays in the allocation of cases to guardians and their heavy workloads. The PLO sets a timescale for the appointment of the Cafcass representative (normally this should have happened within 12 days of the issue of the care proceedings) though experience shows that this has not always been adhered to.

It is essential that you respond efficiently to any queries that the Cafcass representatives have and that you help them conduct their enquiries. Hopefully, difficulties with a Cafcass officer will be rare but if they occur you should discuss this with your manager in the first instance and also your legal department. If difficulties cannot be resolved it is only the court that can authorize the change of appointment.

In *A County Council v K and Others (By the Child's Guardian Ht)* [2011] Sir Nicholas Wall said that the role of Cafcass is to:

> (a) safeguard and promote the welfare of the children, (b) give advice to any court about any application made to it in such proceedings, (c) make provision for the children to be represented in such proceedings, (d) provide information, advice and other support for the children and their families. [38]

For further guidance on the role of the Cafcass officer, see *Child Protection*, in the Focus on Social Work series, by Kim Holt (2014).

Official Solicitor

The Official Solicitor's Office provides services where needed in the justice system to those who are children or adults who lack mental capacity. The Official Solicitor appears as a party in the Court of Protection to advise the court on the best interests of the vulnerable adult. The Official Solicitor also has a role in Family Courts; if a parent lacks mental capacity the Official Solicitor will usually be appointed to represent the parent's best interests in care proceedings.

> KEY CASE ANALYSIS

London Borough of Redbridge v G and Others [2014]

This case provides an example of the role of the Official Solicitor in the Court of Protection. It also illustrates a local authority making an application to the High Court for the protection of an elderly woman considered to be a vulnerable adult and lacking mental capacity. The lady was old and frail and various people had reported concerns that her carers (one of whom was a live-in carer) were exerting undue influence over her. She was represented in the proceedings by the Official Solicitor who also submitted that the lady lacked mental capacity. Her carers, the respondents to the application, submitted that she did not lack capacity.

The lady went to court and sat in court all day for the two days of the hearing. The court heard evidence, including form the social worker and expert witnesses, and concluded she did not have capacity under the provisions of the Mental Capacity Act 2005 and that further investigation would need to be carried out to decide how her best interests would be met 'and her comfort and safety assured'. The judge said:

> Her wishes and feelings will be taken into account at every stage as will her desire to remain in her own home. It is the court's intention that every measure that can be put in place to secure her in her own home is put [in] place. There is an equal need to ensure that she is not overborne or bullied and that she can lead her life as she wants it led. [4]

Expert witnesses

The Expert Witness Institute offers a useful definition:

An expert can be anyone with knowledge of or experience in a particular field or discipline beyond that to be expected of a layman. An expert witness is an expert who makes this knowledge and experience available to a court (or other judicial or quasi-judicial bodies, e.g. tribunals, arbitrations, official enquiries, etc.) to help it understand the issues in a case and thereby reach a sound and just decision.

Expert Witness Institute, undated

Of course, on that definition you as a social worker are an expert in your particular field. However, within your cases the term 'expert witness' will usually be used to mean someone independent of the parties, instructed to report on a technical or scientific matter which is outside the scope of the social worker's expertise. The types of expert witness are limitless, however, in cases about child and adult welfare disciplines frequently called upon are psychiatrists, psychologists, paediatricians, geriatricians and radiologists.

Many local authorities will have their preferred experts. If considering instructing an expert previously unknown to the local authority, you should ask questions about the expert witness.

Box 5.3: Checking the expert witness

1 What are their qualifications?
2 Does the expert have relevant practical experience in the area in issue?
3 Does the expert have experience in litigation of this type? Does he or she prepare reports and attend at trial regularly to give evidence? Only a small percentage of cases proceed to trial and thus an expert who may claim to have been involved in 200 cases may only have given evidence in a few of those cases which could be a disadvantage because the ability to withstand tough cross-examination is essential.
4 Does the expert have sufficient time to deal with the case properly? A good expert will refuse instructions when he or she has insufficient time. The expert will have to spend considerable time examining the papers and the subject-matter of the claim. The expert might also meet and examine the child as part of their assessment, as long as the court gives permission for this.
5 Can the expert be regarded as impartial? There could be reasons not to instruct, such as a conflict of interest arising out of the fact that they have treated or counselled the service user in the past.

The following two cases illustrate the importance of expert evidence; judges aim to prevent overuse of experts but there will be cases where evidence from several experts will be necessary in order that the judge is properly advised.

> → **KEY CASE ANALYSIS** ←
>
> *C v A Local Authority* [2011]
>
> This is an unusual case in that evidence was given at the hearing by a large high number of experts though not an unnecessary proliferation, such were the complexities of the needs of a young man, C, aged 18, with severe autism and severe learning disabilities. He was living at a residential special school. Inadequate care planning and assessment had led to a significant increase in the deprivation of his liberty including his regular seclusion in a 'blue room'. The Official Solicitor took action on behalf of the young man against the local authority which conceded amongst other things 'failure to prepare an appropriate care plan setting out the arrangements for C's care into adulthood including his transfer from the school to a suitable adult placement' and 'failure to complete an assessment and an appropriately detailed pathway plan in time for C's 18th birthday'. As the judge said, it was a 'tragic case'.

Another case, this time from the Family Court, illustrates the importance of expert evidence.

> → **KEY CASE ANALYSIS** ←
>
> *London Borough of Islington v Al Alas and Wray* [2012]
>
> In this case, a child, Jayda, was taken into care by the local authority at birth. By the time she was born her parents had been charged with the murder of her older brother, Jayden. The parents had stood trial at the Old Bailey (the Central Criminal Court) but the judge acceded to the defence application that the case should not be put to the jury and the jury was directed to acquit the parents. In the care proceedings the judge heard four weeks of evidence. The vast majority of the witnesses were clinicians or medical experts because the local authority argued that Jayden had died as a result of non-accidental injury inflicted by the parents and relied on the medical evidence. The expert evidence, though lengthy and complex, proved necessary to assist the judge reaching her conclusion that the balance of the evidence when put together as a whole suggested Jayden's injuries were not caused by trauma.

Special considerations regarding experts in family cases

The test in the Family Procedure Rules for permitting expert evidence used to be whether it was 'reasonably required to resolve the proceedings' but now the expert evidence must be 'necessary to assist the court to resolve the proceedings justly' (s. 13(6) Children and Families Act 2014). This is a more stringent test. What is meant by 'necessary'? In *Re H-L (A Child)* [2013], the President of the Family Division said necessary 'means necessary'. Fortunately, he did elaborate, a little, confirming that necessary 'has a meaning lying somewhere between "indispensable" on the one hand and "useful", "reasonable" or "desirable" on the other hand'. For the expert evidence to be necessary it must be more than 'merely optional or reasonable or desirable'. The overall direction of travel is towards more restricted use of expert evidence and greater reliance on high quality social work opinion.

Clearly, when the case is one such as *London Borough of Islington v Al Alas and Wray* [2012] (above) medical evidence will be necessary. Not all cases require expert medical evidence but, where the court does permit expert evidence in a family case, the parties are encouraged to agree on the expert and jointly instruct the expert. Joint selection is encouraged and may create a less 'confrontational' approach; the expert has an overriding duty to the court and should be objective and independent. Joint instruction is in keeping with the principle that the welfare of the child is paramount; it is not about the parties seeking to win. Notwithstanding the urgency in some cases, expert evidence should not be rushed: 'Justice must never be sacrificed upon the altar of speed.' (*Re NL (A Child) (Appeal: Interim Care Order: Facts And Reasons)* [2014]).

If fewer experts are instructed, social workers are likely to find that their opinions on the best interests of the child (or the vulnerable adult in the case of Court of Protection cases) are scrutinized more closely as they become more central in the case. In 2013, the President of the Family Division, said:

> [o]ne of the problems is that in recent years too many social workers have come to feel undervalued, disempowered and de-skilled ... If the revised PLO is properly implemented one of its outcomes will, I hope, be to re-position social workers as trusted professionals playing the central role in care proceedings which too often of late has

> been overshadowed by our unnecessary use of and reliance upon other experts.
>
> *Munby, 2013a:7*

Independent social workers

An independent social worker (ISW) is a particular type of expert witness. If a party/the parties wish to instruct an ISW to conduct an assessment in a case and submit their findings as evidence, the court will need to be convinced that it is 'necessary'. The court will want to know why the local authority social worker cannot complete the work that it is suggested the ISW undertakes.

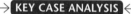

> → **KEY CASE ANALYSIS** ←
>
> *Re Z (A Child: Independent Social Work Assessment)* [2014]
>
> In this case, the judge agreed to adjourning for an ISW assessment even though it would lead to some 'regrettable' further delay. The judge was concerned about the quality of the social work assessment of the father and whether he had been treated fairly. He was also concerned about the quality of the local authority's analysis of the options. In this particular case, a parenting assessment of the father by an ISW was 'necessary' to determine if he could parent the child.

If an application is to be made to instruct an ISW to conduct an assessment and submit a report, the court will want to see their CV, hear why it is necessary to have one instructed and be clear and focused on the issues the ISW should address. The social worker and their manager must be prepared to be closely quizzed on this by a judge who might be thinking that another expert is likely to be unnecessary and to cause unreasonable delay.

As with any proposed assessment that requires another professional to be instructed (such as an ISW or an expert witness), this should be identified as early as possible in legal proceedings to avoid delay that might be harmful and so that your lawyers can seek the necessary permission from the court. If more than one assessment is to be carried out, consider how these might be done alongside each other i.e. concurrently rather than consecutively. There might be resource arguments against concurrent assessment, but once a matter is before the court, a judge will usually want to order concurrent rather than sequential assessments.

Litigants in person

Some people represent themselves at court. They are called litigants in person (LIPs). They may do this because they have no funds for a lawyer, or sometimes they choose to do it themselves. LIPs might or might not have had legal advice from a lawyer, Citizen's Advice Bureau, law centre or independent advice agency. In recognition of the fact that more and more people are representing themselves, the Bar Council, the body that represent barristers, published online *A Guide to Representing Yourself in Court* (2012). It can be found on its website: www.barcouncil.org.uk.

The LIP might cross-examine you at court. Remember they will probably be more nervous than you; there will be a lot at stake for them personally. They might use far more emotive language when questioning you than a lawyer would. Stay calm. It is important that they have their chance to put their version to you and it is also important that you get your chance to respond and disagree if you wish. The judge will be doing his or her best to ensure that the litigant has a fair hearing and that you get your chance to respond. Do not get into an argument with the LIP and try not to take anything personally.

The LIP might be accompanied by a McKenzie friend. This person is not their lawyer and cannot speak for them in court or address the judge. They are there to provide moral support, take notes, help with case papers and quietly give advice to their friend.

And many more

There are many other professionals you may encounter in the legal system. You might meet an ISVA (independent sexual violence adviser), an IDVA (independent domestic violence adviser) or an IMCA (independent mental capacity advocate). In respect of the latter, guidance is set out in *Making Decisions: The Independent Mental Capacity Advocate (IMCA) Service* (OPG, 2007). Though they are called an 'advocate', they are not one in the sense of being someone who is authorized to represent someone in court. They are a supporter.

If you meet someone with a job title that you haven't heard before or you are not sure what their role is, begin a discussion and work out how you can work together effectively.

> ◣ **PRACTICE FOCUS**
>
> A woman with learning disabilities and cerebral palsy alleged an assault by a care worker. The most reliable method of communication she had was to eye point to symbols on an E-tran frame assisted by an RI. (The E-tran frame is 'held by the communication partner 18" in front of the user's face at eye level. The user looks at the place where the letter they wish to communicate is positioned and then to the corresponding colour disc of that letter. The communication partner confirms each letter. If appropriate they can pre-empt the word the user is building up.': see: www.liberator.co.uk/frenchay-e-tran-frame.html.)
>
> The police interview had to be carefully planned and scripted to allow her to answer yes/no/don't know/something else etc. The social worker had previously taken an initial account using leading ways of communication involving suggestions of what might have happened which resulted in discrepancies in accounts.
>
> • What impact might the social worker's actions have on the CPS's decision to prosecute?

Further reading

DfE (2013b) *Working Together to Safeguard Children: A Guide to Inter-agency Working to Safeguard and Promote the Welfare of Children*: this guidance explains how organizations should work together to safeguard children and is essential reading for every child and family social worker.

Johns, R (2014) *Capacity and Autonomy*: this book, also in the Focus on Social Work series, will help you understand adult and child mental capacity issues and why and how good social work practice respects the autonomy of individuals.

6

GIVING CHILDREN AND VULNERABLE ADULTS A VOICE IN THE LEGAL SYSTEM

AT A GLANCE THIS CHAPTER COVERS:

• what social workers can do to help the vulnerable be heard
• a brief history: how the legal system is changing
• special measures for victims and witnesses, including ABE interviews
• ensuring vulnerable suspects and defendants have a voice
• intermediaries – changing the system for good
• special measures and adaptations in the family justice system
• further support and entitlements for witnesses and victims

What social workers can do to help the vulnerable be heard

Not only must a social worker understand the courts and the legal system so that they can present their own best evidence, they must understand how to support their service users to give their best evidence. What is meant by 'give their best evidence'? Simply, it means having the opportunity to offer a complete, accurate and coherent account. It includes a witness being able to say what they want to say, being questioned in a way that they understand and giving answers that can be understood. That is no less than each of us would expect for ourselves in a fair justice system because having your voice heard is a fundamental right.

However, giving evidence, for example, at a police station in an interview or at court from the witness box, is daunting enough even as a professional witness, so consider what it must be like for a parent in care proceedings or a young defendant in a criminal case. Things may be further complicated if the witness feels intimidated because of the nature of the offence (e.g. a knife crime or domestic violence) or has additional communication needs on account of a learning disability or difficulties expressing themselves in English, for example. Whilst it is the judge's job to ensure that the hearing is fair, it is part of the social worker's responsibility to ensure steps have been taken to support their service user to give their best evidence.

A study of 182 children (Plotnikoff and Woolfson, 2009) about their experiences of giving evidence made some shocking discoveries about children's experiences as court. Here are just two quotes from the research report:

> I wish someone had said afterwards 'I realise how difficult it was', but the supporter didn't even say 'Thank you', she just asked me to carry the cups out of the TV link room. They should have sat down with me for five minutes. (Enid, 145)

> They have both seriously changed. They are having nightmares. A feels guilty as he is the eldest and was not able to stop it happening to B. A has gone within himself and B is full of anger – he won't let anyone into his personal space. I asked for help but the social worker told us categorically that the boys could not have counselling before the trial because it would interfere with their evidence. They so needed something in place right there, right then. There was a huge gap – 15 months to wait

for trial. Even now [that the trial is over], no one's offered help. (parent of seven-year-old twins, Alan and Brian)

Plotnikoff and Woolfson, 2009:142

Of course, it is not simply a child witness issue. There are vulnerable adults and vulnerable defendants for whom going to court might be a traumatic experience without appropriate support and assistance from their social worker.

Social workers can play an extremely important role in ensuring proper adjustments are made for the vulnerable. Fortunately, these days police officers, lawyers and judges accept that in order for police investigations and legal proceedings to be fair, adaptations must sometimes be made, such as allowing a supporter or appropriate adult to accompany the witness, using an intermediary to assist with questions and answers and treating a witness's pre-recorded interview as their evidence in chief.

Unfortunately, adaptations are not always well understood (many are still relatively new), witnesses who need them are not always identified by police and lawyers and implementation of special arrangements can be uneven. A well-informed social worker can make all the difference; she can make sure that her service users are treated fairly whether they are a witness or a suspect. This chapter gives examples of special arrangements for vulnerable witnesses and defendants in criminal cases and care proceedings, but the principles can be applied elsewhere, for example, in mental health review tribunals or hearings about special educational needs, in fact in any part of the justice system.

A brief history: how the legal system is changing for victims, witnesses and defendants

Prior to the Youth Justice and Criminal Evidence Act 1999 it was largely left to the trial court to make special allowances to enable children and vulnerable adults to give evidence. The system was ad hoc. It very much depended on the judge's view of what should and could be done and very young children were rarely called as witnesses because the general view prevailed that they were unreliable witnesses.

Today children as young as four sometimes give evidence in criminal trials. This 'includes a number of children who were three when the police interviews were undertaken, some of whom were giving evidence about events that happened when they were two' (Marchant, 2013). Vulnerable and intimidated adults are also beginning to be treated with greater understanding and respect. It is chilling to note that the Mental Health Act 1913 classified those who came under its ambit as 'imbeciles', 'idiots' or 'feeble-minded'. Thankfully, that law is no longer in force. Mental health disorders and other conditions and impairments (dyslexia, Alzheimer's disease, autism and Asperger syndrome, to name but a few) are beginning to be better understood. Obligations for safeguarding children and vulnerable adults apply to the police station and courtroom as well; once vulnerability is identified in a witness or suspect, suitable adjustments should be made. These are discussed below.

The Criminal Justice Act 1991 allowed children for the first time to give evidence in chief via a recording and for the recording to be admitted as direct evidence. In order to provide good practice guidance for those conducting these interviews, in 1992, the Home Office and Department of Health published the 'Memorandum of good practice on video-recorded interviews with children witnesses for criminal proceedings'. 'The memorandum' was superseded by *Achieving Best Evidence* (now simply known as ABE) in 2002. The current version of ABE was issued in 2011 (MoJ, 2011a).

Box 6.1: *MoJ guidance about vulnerable and intimidated witnesses*

1.9 Early identification of the individual abilities as well as disabilities of each vulnerable adult is important in order to guide subsequent planning. An exclusive emphasis upon disability ignores the strengths and positive abilities that a vulnerable individual possesses. Vulnerable witnesses may have had social experiences that could have implications for the investigation and any subsequent court proceedings. For example, if the vulnerable adult has spent a long time in an institutional environment, they may have learned to be compliant or acquiescent. However, such characteristics are not universal and can be ameliorated through appropriate preparation and the use of Special Measures. ...

1.12 Research suggests that the intimidation of witnesses is likely to arise in sexual offences, assaults and those offences where the victim knew the offender and also crimes that involve repeated victimization, such as stalking and racial harassment. In addition, some witnesses to other crimes may be suffering from fear and distress and may require safeguarding and support in order to give their best evidence. ...

- Some witnesses may be vulnerable as well as intimidated (e.g. an elderly victim of vandalism who has dementia on an inner-city estate);
- Others may be vulnerable but not subject to intimidation (e.g. a child who witnesses a robbery in the street); and
- Others may not be vulnerable but may be subject to possible intimidation (e.g. a young woman who fears violence from her current or former partner or someone who has been the subject of a racial attack).

Achieving Best Evidence, MoJ, 2011a

Special entitlements and special measures for victims and witnesses, including the ABE interview

The Code of Practice for Victims

The government signed up to the European Convention on the Rights of Victims of Crime in autumn 2012. This resulted in a review of the *Code of Practice for Victims of Crime*, in force from December 2013 (MoJ, 2013a). The Victims' Minister Damian Green said when the new code was published:

> For too long victims have felt they are treated as an afterthought in the criminal justice system. No more. I am determined that victims are given back their voice and are fully supported. (MoJ, 2013a)

The victim's code gives rights to people who have made allegations that they are victims of crime. These include entitlements to information about how the case is progressing, referrals to organizations supporting victims of crime, making a victim personal statement (VPS) to explain how the crime affected them, seeking a review of CPS decisions not to prosecute etc.

The code provides an overview of the 'victims' journey through the Criminal Justice System' with reference to a flowchart and specifies certain entitlements. Enhanced entitlements are available under the code for victims of the most serious crime, persistently targeted victims and vulnerable or intimidated victims. The code covers **special measures** and highlights the role of RIs. For the purposes of the code, a 'victim' is a person who has suffered harm, including physical, mental or emotional harm or economic loss which was directly caused by criminal conduct or a close relative of a person whose death was directly caused by criminal conduct. If your service user is a victim of a criminal offence, ensure that they know about the code and their entitlements.

Police duties

When they first encounter a person who may be a victim or witness, the police should undertake an assessment of their needs to:

1 establish whether they are a victim of a crime who falls into one or more of the three 'priority' categories (victims of the most serious crime, persistently targeted victims and vulnerable or intimidated victims);
2 in the case of vulnerable or intimidated victims, identify which special measures seem to be most appropriate;
3 inform a variety of decisions that need to be made under the code, including the frequency with which the victim should be updated about the progress of the investigation, whether it is appropriate to suggest/facilitate access to pre-trial therapy etc.

Note: the Advocate's Gateway provides a toolkit on identifying vulnerability in witnesses and defendants and an overview of special measures and adjustments that could and should be made. See The Advocates Gateway (www.theadvocatesgateway.org).

Special measures

If a witness or victim reports a crime to the police they usually have their statement taken down in writing by the police officer. If the matter goes to trial and their statement is disputed they would normally have to go to court to give their version of events from memory from the witness box (evidence in chief) and then they could be challenged on it by the defence (cross-examination).

However, if a witness falls within the eligibility criteria (if they are vulnerable on account of age or impairment or if they are intimidated), the police can interview them on tape/DVD using the ABE guidance. An application is then made for special measures to adduce that interview as the evidence in chief.

'Special measures' is an umbrella term denoting the procedures that adjust the legal process to enable vulnerable witnesses to give their best evidence. The ABE recording of their police interview (often after being edited down for the court hearing) is treated as the witness's evidence in chief; the DVD recording is played in court so that the witness does not have to recount the events, or tell their story, again. This is an example of a special measure. Special measures are contained in an order by a judge which is binding on all the parties and which help to define how a witness will give his or her evidence at the trial. Another example is when the witness is cross-examined over a 'live-link', a closed circuit television link to another room in the court building. The witness does not have to come into the courtroom itself and is seen on a flat screen television screen in the courtroom. Often special measures are used in combination so, for example, the ABE interview is played as evidence in chief and then the witness is cross-examined over live-link. These are just two examples of the special measures that are available.

Key legislation: special measures

The Youth Justice and Criminal Evidence Act 1999 provides special measures for eligible witnesses:

- screening the witness from the accused (s. 23);
- evidence given by live-link (s. 24);
- evidence given in private (s. 25);
- removal of wigs and gowns whilst the witness gives evidence (s. 26);
- video-recorded evidence in chief (s. 27);
- video-recorded cross-examination and re-examination (**section 28**, only piloted in three Crown Courts in 2014 and it remains to be seen if it will be rolled out more widely);
- evidence given through an intermediary (s. 29);*
- use of aids to communications (s. 30).*

Intermediaries and communication aids are only available if the witness is vulnerable. They are not for intimidated witnesses.

Witnesses are eligible for s. 23 to s. 30 special measures if they are under 18 at the time of the hearing or the quality of their evidence is likely to be diminished by reason of a mental disorder or a significant impairment of their social functioning or a physical disability or physical disorder (s. 16). Intimidated witnesses are eligible for the special measures assistance in ss 23 to 28 on the grounds of fear or distress or if they were the victim of a knife crime (s. 17). Section 102 Coroners and Justice Act 2009 provides for a supporter to accompany the witness while giving evidence in the live-link room.

The concept of the vulnerable or intimidated witness really took hold with the introduction of the Youth Justice and Criminal Evidence Act 1999 and its special measures. Special measures became available in July 2002, apart from examination of a witness through an intermediary which came in across England and Wales in 2007. Videoed cross-examination and re-examination was piloted in 2014 in three Crown Courts (Kingston, Leeds and Liverpool).

In order for special measures to be considered, the police officer needs to know or at least to suspect that the witness is vulnerable because of age or incapacity or intimidated because of fear or distress about testifying. Sometimes this is obvious (e.g. when a witness is a child or a rape complainant is distressed about giving her account). Other times disabilities are hidden either because there are no immediately obvious signs (this is sometimes the case with high-functioning autism, for example), symptoms of conditions may be masked or the witness chooses not to reveal their vulnerability.

If you think your service user should be considered for special measures you should speak to them and ask their explicit permission to discuss their vulnerability with the police officer dealing with the case. In the case of a child without capacity to consent, the person with parental responsibility should be asked before you discuss the child's condition with the police officer. The police officer should then discuss with the witness (or the person with parental responsibility) the special measures that are available. Knowing that special measures can be applied for can make the difference between a witness coming forward and having their voice heard or not. It can make the difference between a perpetrator being convicted or not. Whatever the outcome of the case, they can make a huge difference to the witness's experience of the criminal justice system.

As a social worker you might be asked to provide support for a witness at court. You should not agree to do so if you are also a witness in the case. If you stay with the witness while they are giving evidence (either in the police station or at court) you should be given guidance including not to interrupt or intervene during the questioning unless you have a good reason and you must not prompt the witness about what to say. You should not speak to the witness about the case or allow anyone else to do so while the witness is on a break (such as a lunch break or overnight break) during their evidence.

ABE guidance outlines a range of possible tasks for the witness supporter. In some cases you may need to arrange pre-trial therapy or counselling for the witness. There are special CPS rules around this to ensure that the counselling does not interfere with the evidence, but pre-trial counselling is not banned outright as some people think. Your witness supporter role will most likely extend to after the trial and it may be necessary to arrange further counselling or support by others for the witness. You should discuss this with the CPS.

Achieving Best Evidence

Who is the guidance for? The guidance (MoJ, 2011a) is written largely for ABE-trained police interviewers who conduct video-recorded inter-views with victims and witnesses. They are specially trained for the role; in addition they should have their interviews assessed and be quality assured so that they constantly develop their skills. ABE is an important evidence-gathering tool in the police investigation and the recording of the ABE interview may become evidence in a criminal case or in family proceedings.

Is it just about video-recorded interviews? No. ABE is very extensive and covers all sorts of other matters ranging from pre-trial counselling, witness preparation, memory refreshing to the witness supporter role.

Can social workers carry out ABE interviews? Yes, if the social worker is trained and it is agreed as the most appropriate way forward in the police investigation. The police retain their responsibility for the criminal investigation and planning the interview. The decision as to who leads the interview should depend on who is able to establish the best rapport with the witness.

Which witnesses have ABE interviews? 'It applies to both prosecution and defence witnesses' (para. 1.3) who are vulnerable and intimidated witnesses and are therefore eligible for special measures and also signifi-cant witnesses who are not eligible for special measures. (Significant witnesses are also known as 'key' witnesses and are usually in cases where the alleged offence is so serious that it must be heard at the Crown Court. The police may decide that a video-recorded interview, rather than a written record, will give better quality evidence at trial.)

What happens if ABE guidance is not properly followed? ABE says this:

> While it is advisory and does not constitute a legally enforceable code of conduct, practitioners should bear in mind that significant departures from the good practice advocated in it may have to be justified in the courts. (MoJ, 2011a: para. 1.1)

What do judges say about ABE interviews? Judges sometimes decide that the ABE interview in a particular case was so badly conducted or is so unhelpful that the recording, even in its edited form, cannot be used. Therefore, the witness has to give their evidence in chief in person. Sometimes when ABE interviews from criminal cases have been put forward as evidence in Family Court cases, to avoid the child being called as a witness in the family case, Family Court judges have ruled the recording 'inadmissible' because of its poor quality. In addition to special measures, the advocates in the courtroom are also expected to adapt their questioning to the needs of the witness. The Court of Appeal decision in the case of *R v B* [2010] represented a watershed because it established beyond doubt that 'the trial process must cater for the needs of witnesses' and that includes advocates being prepared to modify cross-examination. In *B*, the witness was a four-year-old girl who gave evidence over live-link at the Old Bailey about sexual abuse she had suffered when she was two years old. The Court of Appeal was clear that questioning techniques must be appropriate to the witness's age and level of understanding. In *R v F* [2013], where the witness was a deaf adult, the Court of Appeal reminded advocates that questioning vulnerable witnesses 'requires not only training, flexibility and sensitivity, but also time and patience'.

In 2011 the Advocacy Training Council (ATC) published *Raising the Bar*, the first major research project in England and Wales on how advocates should work with vulnerable people in court. It recommended that 'advocates should be issued with "toolkits" setting out common problems encountered when examining vulnerable witnesses and defendants, together with suggested solutions'. In 2013, the ATC and the Attorney General launched The Advocate's Gateway (the advocatesgateway.org); this website provides case law, research and practical 'toolkits' on questioning vulnerable witnesses. It is freely accessible to all. Toolkits cover identifying vulnerability, planning to question someone with autism, planning to question someone with a learning disability, planning to question someone with a mental disorder or someone who is deaf etc. As well as being of use to advocates and judges, the toolkits are likely to be of use to social workers, police officers and other professionals who work with vulnerable witnesses and defendants.

Ensuring vulnerable suspects and defendants have a voice

PACE codes set out the rights of a suspect and how a suspect should be treated during a police investigation. The codes are issued under the Police and Criminal Evidence Act 1984 (PACE). PACE Code C sets out the requirements for the detention, treatment and questioning of suspects not related to terrorism in police custody. (There is a separate code for suspects related to terrorism.) Code C says that special provision must be made for those under 18 and adults who are suspected to be vulnerable. This includes mental health assessments where appropriate and provision of an appropriate adult at the police station, for example.

If you are the social worker to a child or a mentally disordered or otherwise mentally vulnerable suspect detained for interview at the police station you may find that you are asked to act as their appropriate adult. There are services specifically set up to provide appropriate adults at the police station. You should not agree to be the suspect's appropriate adult if you are a witness to or victim of the alleged offence or if the suspect has made admissions to you about the alleged offence. If you do act as an appropriate adult your role is to provide advice and assistance and you may, for instance, inspect the custody record and consult with the suspect in private. More information is available at the National Appropriate Adult Network (www.appropriateadult.org).

Almost all of the special measures legislation is aimed at witnesses not suspects or defendants; in fact, there has been relatively little development of legislation aimed at protecting their rights in the court process. However, it has been recognized by those who have dealt with defendants that a substantial number are vulnerable. Gregory and Bryan (2011) stated that 'a consensus figure of 50–60% of young people who are involved in offending having speech, language and communication needs is emerging'.

Apart from s. 47 Police and Justice Act 2006 which allows certain accused to give evidence through a live-link, there is no legislation in force which permits the use of special measures for defendants. Section 104 of the Coroners and Justice Act 2009 provides for examination through an intermediary of a vulnerable accused at their oral evidence-giving, but it is not yet in force. Despite the lack of legislation judges have allowed special measures for vulnerable defendants.

In *C v Sevenoaks Youth Court* [2009] the defendant C was a 12-year-old boy with complex mental health issues. The court held that:

> when trying a young child, and most particularly a child such as 'C' who is only 12 with learning and behavioural difficulties, notwithstanding the absence of any express statutory power, the Youth Court has a duty under the inherent powers and under the Criminal Procedure Rules to take such steps as are necessary to ensure that he has a fair trial, not just during the proceedings, but beforehand as he and his lawyers prepare for the trial.
>
> C v Sevenoaks Youth Court [2009]:[17]

The principle was reiterated in 2011 in *R on the Application of AS v Great Yarmouth Youth Court* where magistrates had seen no reason to allow the use of an intermediary for a defendant with attention deficit and hyper-activity disorder who would concentrate not on the questions being asked of him but on those previously asked and so would appear not to be engaging properly with each question. The case was sent back to the magistrates to be heard again.

Intermediaries – changing the system for good

Under the special measures regime of the Youth Justice and Criminal Evidence Act 1999 where vulnerable witnesses are 'eligible for assistance on the grounds of age or incapacity', the most innovative special measure is the intermediary. Their function is to help communicate questions put to the witness and answers given by the witness in reply to them. They can explain the questions or answers as necessary to enable them to be understood by the witness or the questioner.

Ten steps in the intermediary role

1 Police officer identifies the witness has communication needs and that an intermediary might be required.
2 Police officer agrees with the CPS that a registered intermediary (RI) should be requested.
3 An MoJ RI is requested from the matching service (the Witness Intermediary Scheme (WIS) Matching Service is managed by the National Crime Agency on behalf of the MoJ; 0845 0005463)
4 An intermediary with the necessary expertise in the communication need (e.g. autism/deafness/learning disability/mental health) comes and meets the police officer and assesses the witness.
5 The intermediary advises the police officer how best to conduct the ABE interview.
6 The intermediary sits in on the ABE interview assisting with communication issues e.g. suggesting that the officer check that the witness understands the meaning of a particular word.
7 The intermediary writes a report for court.
8 The intermediary attends court with the witness to help with communication at the witness's court familiarization visit.
9 Shortly before the witness gives evidence, the intermediary, judge and advocates in the trial agree the 'ground rules' for the questioning of the witness (this takes place at what is known as the ground rules hearing).
10 The intermediary attends trial, sitting alongside the witness, advising the judge and advocates if communication breaks down or if a ground rule is broken.

In 2007, after a successful pilot, the WIS was rolled out across England and Wales to all 43 police forces and in CPS areas. There are currently approximately 100 RIs operating from an MoJ register. When a police officer identifies that the witness might benefit from the assistance of an RI the officer should speak to the CPS to discuss the possible involvement of an RI in a case. If agreed, the police officer then contacts the witness intermediary team with a request and the team will endeavour to match the witness's needs to an RI with suitable expertise, operating in the geographical area of the witness and available on the dates required.

The police should obtain the necessary consents from the witness (or from the person with parental responsibility which may be the social worker if the child is under a care order or interim care order) so that the RI can look at relevant reports and speak to professionals (teachers, for example) about the witness's communication needs and abilities.

The RI conducts an assessment of the witness's communication abilities and needs. A third party must be present: this could be the social worker, for example, but is usually the interviewing police officer. The RI provides a preliminary report for the interviewing police officer to help them plan communication in the ABE interview. The RI only intervenes in the ABE interview if the officer needs help communicating with the witness. They are not a witness supporter nor are they a second interviewing officer.

Next the RI writes a report for the court based on their assessment, other information gathered about the witness, and what they learned about the witness's communication needs during the interview. The judge later hears the application for the use of the intermediary who may attend trial as well to assist with communication with the witness. The RI can also attend the court familiarization visit to assist with communication. They can also advise the Witness Service on matters relating to the witness's welfare. They can assist while a witness gets to know the live-link room and practises speaking and listening to questions over the live-link (of course, the evidence in the case must not be discussed).

The RI can advise on timetabling of the witness's evidence so, for example, they might advise that the witness would be at their best first thing in the morning. They also advise when and how the witness can watch their ABE interview DVD (which may be long and the witness might need breaks) to refresh their memory. Contrary to what some people at court think, there is no rule that says the witness should view their interview at the same time as the jury. The important thing is that they have the opportunity to refresh their memory from it before they are cross-examined.

Before the witness gives evidence the intermediary must be part of a ground rules hearing with the trial judge and the advocates in order to agree all the matters regarding the manner of the witness giving evidence. The outcomes will be based on the RI's report recommendations. When ground rules are agreed well enough in advance of the hearing, this allows the advocate to properly plan the questioning and the court can ensure that technical and practical issues are resolved in good time for when the witness gives evidence.

The RI, having taken the intermediary oath, assists during the giving of evidence. They sit alongside the witness in the live-link room (or stand next to them if they are giving evidence in court) in order to monitor communication. They intervene during questioning when appropriate and as often as appropriate in accordance with the ground rules and the recommendations in their report.

Even if the witness has not had an intermediary at an ABE interview, it does not necessarily mean that one is not needed at trial. It may be necessary to make a late application because the witness's communication needs have gone unnoticed until the trial. Even if there is no intermediary for a vulnerable witness there should be a ground rules hearing so that the judge and the advocates have an agreed understanding about how the trial process will be modified (including the questioning) to take into account the witness's needs.

> KEY CASE ANALYSIS

R v Watts [2010]

In *R v Watts* [2010], intermediaries assisted vulnerable adults to give evidence to the police about abuse in their care home. The defendant was convicted.

> The four complainants were residents in the same residential care home at which the **appellant** was a part-time worker. All four women were profoundly disabled and wheelchair bound, three with cerebral palsy, and one tetraplegic with an acquired brain injury.
>
> The use of intermediaries forms an integral part of the structure of the special measures regime. In the present case ... two of the complainants gave evidence with the assistance of an intermediary (one of whom was not registered) by means of a process which was seen by the jury. [18]

Social workers should note that not all police officers will identify a witness's vulnerability and, even when they do, they might not be aware of the benefits of using an intermediary. ABE interviews do not always result in disclosures if the right communication strategies are not put in place for that particular witness. Social workers may need to tactfully suggest: 'Have you considered using an intermediary?'

PRACTICE FOCUS

Imagine you are at the Crown Court supporting your service user, a 15-year-old who is the subject of a care order. She was nine at the time of the alleged offence, a rape by her uncle. The prosecutor says that he has worked with intermediaries before and that in each case the intermediary has not had to intervene, so in fact the intermediary probably isn't really needed. The prosecutor asks if you wouldn't mind staying to support the witness in the live-link room so that he can send the intermediary away. Your service user has not previously had a court familiarization visit.

- What would you say to the prosecutor?
- Your 15-year-old service user asks you: 'Is the barrister going to try to confuse me and shout at me?' What would you say to your service user?

Special measures and adaptations in the family justice system

Children and vulnerable adults can also be witnesses in the Family Courts. We do not know precisely how many parents in care proceedings would be classed as vulnerable, however, social workers will know from experience that it is not unusual for parents involved in care proceedings to have mental health disorders or learning difficulties or to be vulnerable in other ways. Swift et al. (2013) found 'evidence which indicates that parents with learning disabilities are often unsupported in their involvement with child protection agencies or courts'. The Family Justice Council/Nuffield Foundation sobering report *Parental Perspectives on the Family Justice System in England and Wales: A Review of Research* concluded that:

> [p]arents find the whole experience of going to court traumatic and alienating … greater attention needs to be paid to the needs of parents caught up in court proceedings, and most particularly to the needs of especially vulnerable groups such as parents with learning difficulties or mental health problems, women who have experienced domestic violence, and parents from minority ethnic communities.
>
> *Hunt, 2010:119*

Special arrangements can be made for adults in the Family Courts and applications are also made to call children as witnesses in family cases.

Family Courts are not set up with special measures facilities such as live-links and screens. They have to borrow them from the criminal courts or make other arrangements. As unsatisfactory as that may seem, it is the way things are and the way they will be unless and until money is available to invest in this aspect of the family justice system, however, this should not prevent you discussing with the lawyers what arrangements can be put in place to assist vulnerable witnesses. As the Court of Appeal said in *Re M* (below), the overriding duty of the court is to ensure that there is a fair trial.

> → **KEY CASE ANALYSIS** ←

Re M (Oral Evidence: Vulnerable Witness) [2012]

In this case, a father's appeal against a fact-finding decision was successful on the ground that inadequate special measures were in place when he gave evidence. The father was of 'limited capacity' and a report recommended a number of things to support him giving evidence including 'an advocate or intermediary in order to help him to negotiate and understand the court processes and proceedings'. On the day of the hearing there was no screen, live-link or intermediary for the father.

Despite the father's counsel applying to adjourn, the judge decided to press on. The Court of Appeal described what had happened as 'an unsatisfactory makeshift' arrangement, the guardian having stepped in to take on the role of intermediary. The Court of Appeal noted the pressure that the judge would have been under to avoid adjourning and the ensuing months of delay but 'that general duty [to avoid delay and achieve targets] cannot in any circumstance override the duty to ensure that any litigant in her court receives a fair trial and is guaranteed what support is necessary to compensate for disability'.

At the rehearing support for the father included an independent, qualified intermediary.

When it comes to children giving evidence in family cases, there is no longer a presumption that they should not. In the Supreme Court in *Re W (Children)* [2010], Lady Hale said that, when considering whether the child should be a witness, 'the court will have to weigh two considerations: the advantages that that will bring to the determination of the truth and the damage it may do to the welfare of this or any other child'. She suggested ways in which the court could hear children's evidence and minimize the potential harm.

> One possibility is an early video'd cross examination as proposed by Pigot. Another is cross-examination via video link. But another is putting the required questions to her through an intermediary. This could be in the court itself, as would be common in continental Europe and used to be much more common than it is now in the courts of this country.
>
> Re W (Children) *[2010]:[28]*

In 2011 the Family Justice Council issued *Guidelines in Relation to Children Giving Evidence in Family Proceedings*. It recommended that an intermediary should be considered at the earliest opportunity and provided detailed suggestions as to how a child's evidence might be facilitated in a family hearing.

Ideally, for all vulnerable witnesses, an intermediary would be assigned at the earliest opportunity so that they can assess the witness, report to court and be at the hearing when the witness is giving evidence. In South Africa, for example, some child witnesses give their evidence via an intermediary in a separate room which is linked to the courtroom by closed circuit television but, unlike UK court live-links, the child does not see or hear anything that happens in court. The court can see and hear what happens in the live-link room and the intermediary hears the questions through earphones. The intermediary translates questions for the child into suitable language but without changing the purpose of the question. Obtaining an intermediary for a Family Court case is not always easy. Unfortunately, courts do not have intermediary budgets. Applications for intermediaries have been known to get stuck in funding negotiations between local authorities and the legal aid funders.

On-the-spot question

If you were the social worker for the child due to be called as a witness in family proceedings, what special arrangements could be put in place? (Remember the Family Courts are not limited to applying the special measures of the criminal courts.)

Further support and entitlements for witnesses and victims in criminal cases

Any witness, vulnerable or otherwise can benefit from the support offered by Victim Support.

It is 'the national charity giving free and confidential help to victims of crime, witnesses, their family, friends and anyone else affected across England and Wales'. Victim Support runs the Witness Service which, amongst other things, provides pre-trial court familiarization visits. Witnesses who are due to give evidence over live-link should be able to go to the live-link room and practise using the live-link (the evidence in the actual case must not be discussed or rehearsed).

You can direct your service users to www.victimsupport.org.uk or its helpline on 0845 30 30 900 for support.

In December 2013 the government published the *Witness Charter: Standards of Care for Witnesses in the Criminal Justice System* (MoJ, 2013d). Available on the internet, it sets out how a witness can expect to be treated by the police if they are a witness to a crime or incident, and if they are asked to give evidence in a criminal court.

Further reading

Marchant, R (2012) 'How young is too young? The evidence of children under five in the English criminal justice system' (2013) *Child Abuse Review*, www.wileyonlinelibrary.com DOI: 10.1002/car.2273 – this article dispels the myths that very young children cannot give reliable evidence about the harm that they have suffered.

The Advocate's Gateway provides practical advice aimed at advocates. It is already widely used by practitioners in many fields who want access to succinct guidance that will help them communicate with those who are vulnerable on account of their communication needs. Guidance covers identifying vulnerability, deafness, use of live-link, autism, learning disabilities, mental disorders etc. The website also includes the training film *A Question of Practice* which shows how an RI works at court. www.theadvocatesgateway.org

7

DEALING WITH OUTCOMES: THE RESULTS AND THE AFTERMATH OF COURT HEARINGS

AT A GLANCE THIS CHAPTER COVERS:

- after giving evidence
- making sense of court decisions
- media
- tweeting, blogging etc.
- future reforms

After giving evidence

If you prepared well, you should be able to walk away from the witness box feeling you did your best. You may not have liked the experience but you should at least feel that you have had your chance to say what you saw, what you heard and what you did and been able answer questions and challenges that came by way of cross-examination.

There will be a decision from the court, but how long it takes for it to arrive depends on a number of things. If it is a jury they will return a verdict within hours or days or they will indicate that they are unable to reach a verdict (they are a 'hung' jury), in which case the jury is 'discharged'.

If it is a decision being made by a judge as opposed to a jury, sometimes the judge will give a decision there and then (an '*ex tempore*' judgment). On other occasions you will have to wait for a 'reserved' judgment. It may be given weeks, days or months later – usually it is weeks. If the judgment is reserved, it is often handed out at court as a typewritten document at a later date rather than read out.

It will either be a decision that gives reasons (a judgment in a family or civil case) or one that does not (a verdict in a criminal case). Reasons when given might tell you what the court thought of your evidence. In any event, on hearing the 'result' you will probably reflect on whether you were believed or not. But before you begin to feel either elated or depressed, consider that decision-making based on watching and listening to a witness is not an accurate science. The judge or jury does its best but, as yet, we do not have a foolproof way to determine which witness (if any) is giving the most complete, accurate and coherent account.

By all means ask a colleague to come to court with you and give you feedback after you have given evidence. Take on board their comments and the court's as well if they make mention of your evidence. Eventually, with enough experience you might even begin to enjoy the process of giving evidence, after all the purpose is to help the court and that is important and necessary. But remember, the system is not perfect and you can only do your best. If you prepare well, act with integrity and tell the truth you will have done what is required of you as a witness.

Making sense of court decisions

Court orders are not always easy to understand. They may be delivered quickly, they may not be audible other than to those sitting closest to the judge, and they may be in what seems like an impenetrable legal language. Part of a lawyer's job is to explain the outcome of the hearing to their client. If you are not at court with a lawyer, find a member of the court staff and ask what the outcome was.

In subsequent meetings with your service user you need to be able to understand and possibly explain again to them what happened. Make sure that you understand and that all necessary steps have been taken to ensure that your service user understands. Communication disabilities must be catered for both at and after hearings.

> **KEY CASE ANALYSIS**

Re C (A Child) (Guidance on Proceedings Involving Profoundly Deaf Parent) [2014]

In this case, the court issued guidance on the approach to be taken by professionals, local authorities, legal advisors, the court service and judges in cases involving a parent or parents who were profoundly deaf. In such a case there:

> should be expert and insightful analysis and support provided by a suitably qualified person at every stage. The ordinary understanding was that sign language was sign language, but there were differences between British Sign Language and English Supported Sign Language. A person might use any combination of those or their own version personal to them. There was an opportunity to use deaf relay interpretation.

The court made it clear that this is not simply about good practice; the courts, local authorities and Cafcass have a duty to function within the terms of the Equality Act 2010 [36].

The Advocate's Gateway contains advice in the form of a toolkit for those wishing to communicate with those who are deaf.

Verdicts in criminal cases are simply 'guilty' or 'not guilty'. Reasons are not given with them. Note that not guilty is not a verdict of 'innocent' – there is no such thing. Every person is innocent until proven guilty but a verdict of not guilty does not prove innocence.

Victims of violent offences may be eligible for compensation from the Criminal Injuries Compensation Authority (CICA). If you are the social worker to a child who is in the care of the local authority and you think that the child may be eligible, speak to the local authority legal department. It may be your responsibility to make the claim on behalf of the child. The CICA has a website and can be contacted on 0800 358 3601.

Winning or losing?

In our adversarial system it can feel like a competition to win, but in your professional capacity as a social worker it is not about winning or losing. It is about responding to the decision of the court in the most appropriate way. The local authority may or may not have obtained the result it sought. You should have already prepared the next steps whatever the outcome. Does it mean a change of placement because the care order was sought but was not granted? Does someone, e.g. a foster carer, need to be informed immediately of the court outcome?

Although your own response may be calm, your service user's might not be. That may be understandable. Imagine it was an application by the local authority to dispense with the parent's consent to adoption of their child? The parent's and the birth family's lives will be irrevocably changed against the parent's wishes if the court grants the local authority application. Hopefully, their lawyers will be there at court to explain the outcome, advise them on what happens next and ensure they get the necessary support. On rare occasions, people get so fraught that threats are made. If you witness this or are on the receiving end of this, report it to your lawyers and the court staff. Security officers operate in court buildings and might need to be put on notice. On one occasion, a social worker was threatened at court and dismissed it. Later that threat turned into physical violence but the security staff were elsewhere in the building. With hindsight, she should have discretely warned the security staff that something might occur so that they could have been close by.

If you are unhappy about the result and think that the court got it wrong, discuss this with your lawyer. An appeal may be possible but it is not a re-hearing. The court that hears the appeal is not there to substitute its own decision for that of the judge below, but it can rectify a mistake in law or procedure by a lower court. In order for there to be certainty and finality there are time limits on bringing appeals. Once again your lawyer will advise you on these if you are considering or responding to an appeal.

Media

The rules about media reporting vary from case to case. Check the position with your lawyer before revealing anything to the media.

Though the criminal courts tend to be the most open ('justice must be seen to be done'), sometimes there are reporting restrictions. This could be to protect the identity of a vulnerable victim (e.g. in a rape case) or a child witness or defendant. Take care not to inadvertently reveal information – don't for instance discuss sensitive information on the phone in public areas at court. The Leveson Inquiry (DCMS/Leveson, 2012) and the activities of some journalists (e.g. in the Milly Dowler case) demonstrate previous unethical and illegal behaviour to get a 'scoop'. If you have access to a press office, direct all media enquiries through its staff and make sure that they are also liaising with the local authority legal department.

In the Family Courts, accredited media may report certain aspects of the case but not usually the names of the people concerned, however, the usual wording at the top of Family Court judgments is:

> The judgment is being distributed on the strict understanding that in any report no person other than the advocates or the solicitors instructing them (and other persons identified by name in the judgment itself) may be identified by name or location and that in particular the anonymity of the children and the adult members of their family must be strictly preserved.

The Court of Protection judgments are usually similarly headed, as follows, at the top of the first page and in red so as not to be missed:

> The Judgment is being distributed on the strict understanding that in any report no person other than the advocates or solicitors instructing them and other persons identified by name in the judgment itself may be identified by name or location and that in particular the anonymity of 'C' and his family must be strictly preserved.

In *Re E* [2013] these words were used so as to allow for greater transparency and media reporting *in that particular case*:

> This does not prevent the parents from identifying themselves and the child in the event that they wish to discuss and/or publicise what has happened to them and their family in the course of these proceedings and beforehand. (Judgment Headnote)

The case concerned local authority failings in a child protection case and the usual family case restrictions on publicity about the judgment were not applied in this case.

> **KEY CASE ANALYSIS**

A v Independent News & Media Ltd and Others [2010]

The courts have also highlighted the need for privacy in relation to people whose affairs are considered in the Court of Protection. In *A v Independent News & Media Ltd and Others* [2010] the then Lord Chief Justice said:

> The affairs of those who are not incapacitated are, of course, decided and handled privately, usually at home, sometimes with, but usually without confidential professional advice. None of these decisions is the business of anyone other than the individual or individuals who are making them. And that, as we emphasise, represents an entirely simple, and we suggest self-evident aspect of personal autonomy. The responsibility of the Court of Protection arises just because the reduced capacity of the individual requires interference with his or her personal autonomy.
>
> The new statutory structure starts with the assumption that just as the conduct of their lives by adults with the necessary mental capacity is their own affair, so too the conduct of the affairs of those adults who are incapacitated is private business. Hearings before the Court of Protection should therefore be held in private unless there is good reason why they should not. In other words, the new statutory arrangements mirror and rearticulate one longstanding common law exception to the principle that justice must be done in open court. [19]

In January 2014 the President of the Family Division, Sir James Munby, issued new guidelines about the publication of judgments in Family Court and Court of Protection cases with the aim of creating greater transparency (Practice Guidance, 2014a; 2014b). Publication of the judgments, which may be heavily anonymized, is not the same as putting all the details of the case in the public domain. Always check with your legal advisers to ensure that you understand the limitations if any on disclosing anything about the case that you are involved in.

Tweeting, blogging etc.

On 4 December 2013 the government announced that, in future, advisory notes from the Attorney General will be published to help prevent social media users from committing a contempt of court. Previously, the advice had been issued only to publishers and media organizations. The Attorney General Dominic Grieve QC MP said:

> Blogs and social media sites like Twitter and Facebook mean that individuals can now reach thousands of people with a single tweet or post. This is an exciting prospect, but it can pose certain challenges to the criminal justice system ... I hope that by making this information available to the public at large, we can help stop people from inadvertently breaking the law, and make sure that cases are tried on the evidence, not what people have found online.
>
> *Attorney General, 2013*

Tweeting, blogging or similar about any of your cases can take you into a legal minefield whether or not there are already proceedings. Get legal advice if you are thinking about making any public comments.

Future legal reforms for social workers

The most significant court reforms on the immediate horizon in family justice are contained in the Children and Families Act 2014. It includes measures on:

- adoption and children (it aims to tackle delay);
- a new 26-week time limit for care proceedings;
- children and young people with special educational needs (changes to assessing needs and special provision);
- statutory rights to leave and pay for parents and adopters;
- time off work for ante-natal care;
- the right to request flexible working etc.

Will the 26-week time limit for completion of care proceedings place unrealistic pressures on social workers? Or will it reduce the pressure on social workers because proceedings will not drag on so long? Will greater control of expert witness evidence and reduction in the use of experts mean that social workers' opinion evidence becomes more respected?

Sir James Munby, the President of the Family Division and President of the Court of Protection, said in October 2013 (Jordan's Court of Protection Practice and Procedure Conference, London, 16 October 2013) that, with the family reforms nearing conclusion, he would be turning his attention to reform of the Court of Protection.

More change comes in the form of the Care Act 2014, aimed at safeguarding adults from abuse or neglect.

Time will tell how these reforms impact on social workers. However, the main purpose of the law remains to improve people's lives.

USEFUL WEBSITES

www.bailii.org
The British and Irish Legal Information Institute provides free access to British and Irish case law and legislation, European Union case law, Law Commission reports and other law-related British and Irish material.

www.ico.org.uk
The Information Commissioner's website has lots of useful guidance on data security and advice on handling personal data properly.

www.justice.gov.uk
The MoJ website contains a wide range of information from the latest court rules and practice directions to statistics on judicial diversity as well as information for court users.

www.scie.org.uk
The website of the Social Care Institute for Excellence provides training and guidance including on keeping case notes, taking minutes of meetings, report-writing etc.

www.theadvocatesgateway.org
This website has guidance aimed at advocates but is useful for anyone who wishes to know how to support vulnerable witnesses and defendants. This website includes specific guidance on how to question those with communication needs.

GLOSSARY

Adversarial
A word used to describe the system of justice in England and Wales; it is a system which generally pitches one side against another, each putting forward a version of events, as opposed to having a judge-led inquiry to investigate the facts.

Advocate
Within the legal profession, this refers to a person who is has the right to speak on behalf of their client in court. He or she may be a solicitor or a barrister and will put forward arguments and can question witnesses.

Appellant
The side appealing a decision of the court.

Applicant
The side which is applying for a court order, e.g. the local authority is the applicant when it applies for a care order.

Claimant
The side (a person or an organization) bringing a claim (usually for damages in money) under civil law, e.g. a local authority service user sues for breach of his/her humans rights.

Cross-examination
When a witness's testimony is challenged by the other side with the aim of undermining that evidence or enhancing their own case. Leading questions are often used.

Defendant
The side (a person or an organization) defending a legal action.

Evidence
What is placed before the court in order to prove a matter that is disputed. Witness evidence may be oral or written or evidence may be in the form of

an inanimate object such as a drawing, photograph or closed circuit television footage.

Examination in chief
The process by which a witness gives their version of events (their oral testimony) in response to questions asked by the advocate who called him or her to the stand. Usually the questions are not leading, that is they will start with who, when, what, why, where or how.

Intermediary
A person who facilitates communication so that questions to the witness may be understood by the witness and answers they give are complete, accurate and coherent.

Judgment
The decision of the judge setting out the facts, the relevant law and conclusions reached by the court. Note that it is correctly spelt with just one 'e' in the context of court judgments as opposed to a professional 'judgement' for example.

Lawyer
A general, umbrella term describing a person qualified to advise on the law. It includes barristers and solicitors.

Live-link
A system allowing a witness to give oral evidence from a location away from the courtroom linked to the courtroom via closed circuit television.

President, The
The President of the Family Division, the most senior Family Court judge in England and Wales and also the President of the Court of Protection.

Re-examination
The option given to the party that called the witness to put additional questions to clarify anything said in cross-examination.

Respondent
The side (a person or an organization) responding to an application for a court order or declaration, e.g. a parent is a respondent to an application for a care order in respect of their child.

Special measures
Adjustments made by the court to ensure that proceedings are fair for those who are intimidated or vulnerable by virtue of their age or incapacity. These

include the use of screens around the witness, live-link, removal of wigs and gowns and the use of intermediaries.

Section 28
Refers to the powers of the criminal courts to pre-record the cross-examination of a vulnerable witness. This is a special measure (s. 28 Youth Justice and Criminal Evidence Act 1999).

Witness
A person who is called to give evidence at a hearing in a court or tribunal.

Witness familiarization
Preparation which allows a witness to become familiar with the process of giving evidence with the aim of enabling them to give their best evidence.

BIBLIOGRAPHY

All Party Parliamentary Group on Social Work (2013) *Inquiry into the State of Social Work* (Birmingham: British Association of Social Workers)

ATC (2011) *Raising the Bar: The Handling of Vulnerable Witnesses, Victims and Defendants in Court* (London: ATC)

ATC (2013) www.theadvocatesgateway.org

Attorney General (2013) *Attorney General's Guidelines on Disclosure for Investigators, Prosecutors and Defence Practitioners 2013* (London: Attorney General's Office)

Attorney General's Office (2013) 'Attorney General to warn Facebook and Twitter users about contempt of court' Press Release 4 December 2013

Bar Council (2012) *A Guide to Representing Yourself in Court* (London: Bar Council) www.barcouncil.org.uk/media/203109/srl_guide_final_for_online_use.pdf

Bichard, M (2004) *The Bichard Inquiry Report* (Norwich: HMSO)

Boylan Kemp, J (2011) *English Legal System: The Fundamentals* (London: Sweet & Maxwell)

Brammer, A (2009) *Social Work Law* (London: Longman)

Brammer, A (2011) 'Law and social work' in K Wilson, G Ruch, M Lymbery and A Cooper (eds), *Social Work: An Introduction to Contemporary Practice* (London: Longman)

Brammer, A and P Cooper (2011) 'Still waiting for a meeting of minds: child witnesses in the criminal and family justice systems' 12 *Criminal Law Review* 925–41

Brayne, H and H Carr (2013) *Law for Social Workers* (Oxford: OUP)

Carlile, Lord (2012) *The Edlington Case: A Review by Lord Carlile of Berriew CBE QC* (London: Department for Education)

Civil Justice Council (2005, amended 2009) *Protocol for the Instruction of Experts to Give Evidence in Civil Claims* (London: Civil Justice Council) www.justice.gov.uk/courts/procedure-rules/civil/contents/form_section_images/practice_directions/pd35_pdf_eps/pd35_prot.pdf

Cooper, P (2011a) 'Child witnesses in family proceedings: should intermediaries be showing us the way?' 41 *Family Law* 397–403

Cooper, P (2011b) 'ABE interviews, children's testimony and hearing the voice of the child in family cases: are we barking up the right tree?' in M Thorpe and W Tyzack (eds), *Dear David: A Memo to the Norgrove Committee from the Dartington Conference 2011* (London: Jordan) 23–31

Cooper, P (2012) *Tell Me What's Happening 3: Registered Intermediary Survey 2011* (London: City University)

Cooper, P (2013) 'Witness competency hearings – a test of competence' 2 *Criminal Bar Quarterly* 5

Cooper, P (2014) 'Speaking when they are spoken to: vulnerable witnesses in care proceedings' 26(2) *Child and Family Law Quarterly* 132–51

Cooper, P and D Wurtzel (2013) 'A day late and a dollar short: in search of an intermediary scheme for vulnerable defendants in England and Wales' 1 *Criminal Law Review* 4–22

Cooper, P and D Wurtzel (2014) 'Better the second time around? Department of Justice Registered Intermediaries Schemes and lessons from England and Wales' 65(1) *Northern Ireland Legal Quarterly* 39–61

Coventry Local Safeguarding Children Board (2013) *Serious Case Review Re Daniel Pelka* (Coventry: Coventry LSCB) www.coventrylscb.org.uk/files/SCR/FINAL%20Overview%20Report%20%20DP%20130913%20Publication%20version.pdf

Cover, M (2012) 'O Guardian, Where Art Thou?' 49 (spring) *Association of Lawyers for Children Newsletter* 2–6

CPS (2013a) *Code for Crown Prosecutors* (London: CPS)

CPS (2013b) Protocol and Good Practice Model Disclosure of Information in Cases of Alleged Child Abuse and Linked Criminal and Care Directions hearings www.cps.gov.uk/publications/docs/third_party_protocol_2013.pdf

Darbyshire, P (2011) *Sitting in Judgment: The Working Lives of Judges* (Oxford: Hart)

Darbyshire, P (2013) *Nutshells: English Legal System* 9th edn (London: Sweet & Maxwell)

DCMS/Leveson, Justice (2012) *Leveson Inquiry: Report into the Culture, Practices and Ethics of the Press* (London: DCMS)

DCSF (2008) *Information Sharing: Guidance for Practitioners and Managers* (London: DCSF)

DfE (2013a) *The Government's Response to Lord Carlile's report on the Edlington Case* (London: DfE)

DfE (2013b) *Working Together to Safeguard Children: A Guide to Inter-agency Working to Safeguard and Promote the Welfare of Children* (London: DfE)

Dickens, J (2013) *Social Work, Law and Ethics* (Abingdon: Routledge)

DoH (2013) *Statement of Government Policy on Adult Safeguarding* (London: DoH)

Du Cann, R (1993) *The Art of the Advocate* (London: Penguin)

Eekelaar, J and M Maclean (2013) *Family Justice: The Work of Family Judges in Uncertain Times* (Oxford: Hart)

Essex County Council (2013) 'Essex County Council responds to interest in story headlined "Essex removes baby from mother"' 2 December www.essex.gov.uk/News/Pages/Essex-County-Council-responds-to-interest-in-story-headlined-Essex-removes-baby-from-mother.aspx

Expert Witness Institute (undated) *What is an Expert Witness?* www.ewi.org.uk/membership_directory/whatisanexpertwitness

Family Justice Council (2011) *Guidelines in Relation to Children Giving Evidence in Family Proceedings* (London: Family Justice Council)

Freeman, C (2013) 'Child taken from womb by caesarean then put into care' *Daily Telegraph* 30 November www.telegraph.co.uk/news/uknews/law-and-order/10486452/Child-taken-from-womb-by-caesarean-then-put-into-care.html

Girl A and N Bunyan (2013) *My Story: The Truth about the Rochdale Sex Ring by the Victim Who Stopped Them* (London: Ebury Press)

Gregory, J and K Bryan (2011) 'Speech and language therapy intervention with a group of persistent and prolific young offenders in a non-custodial setting with previously undiagnosed speech, language and communication difficulties' 46(2) *International Journal of Language and Communication Disorders* 202–15

Gudjonsson, G (2010) 'Psychological vulnerabilities during police interviews. Why are they important?' *Legal and Criminological Psychology* 15

Haringey Local Safeguarding Children Board (2009) *Serious Case Review: Baby Peter* (London: Haringey LSCB)

Heaton-Armstrong, A, E Shephers, G Gudjonsson and D Wolchover (eds) (2006), *Witness Testimony* (Oxford: OUP)

Henderson, E and F Seymour (2013) *Expert Witnesses under Examination in the New Zealand Criminal and Family Courts* (Auckland: University of Auckland with the New Zealand Law Foundation)

HM Government (2003) *Every Child Matters* Cm 5860 (Norwich: TSO)

Holt, K (2014) *Child Protection* (Basingstoke: Palgrave Macmillan)

House of Commons Select Committee (2003) *Select Committee Report, Sixth Report of Session 2002–2003, The Victoria Climbié Inquiry Report* (London: TSO)

Hostettler, J (2006) *Fighting for Justice: The History and Origins of the Adversarial Trial* (Winchester: Waterside Press)

Hunt, J (2010) *Parental Perspectives on the Family Justice System in England and Wales: A Review of Research* (London: Family Justice Council/Nuffield Foundation)

Judge, the Right Honourable the Lord (2013) 'Half a century of change: the evidence of child victims' Toulmin Lecture in Law and Psychiatry, March 2013

Judicial College (2012) *Judicial College Bench Checklist: Young Witness Cases* (London: Judicial College)

Johns, R (2014) *Capacity and Autonomy* (Basingstoke: Palgrave Macmillan)

Kelly, C (2004) *Serious Case Review: Ian Huntley, North East Lincolnshire 1995–2001* (Grimsby: North East Lincolnshire Area Child Protection Committee)

Laming, Lord (2003) *The Victoria Climbié Inquiry* (London: TSO) www.official-documents.gov.uk/document/cm57/5730/5730.pdf

Laming, Lord (2009) *The Protection of Children in England: A Progress Report* (London: TSO)

Loftus, E (2006) *Witness Testimony: Psychological, Investigative and Evidential Perspectives* (Oxford: Oxford University Press)

Loftus, E (2013) 'Elizabeth Loftus: The fiction of memory' on TED talks www.ted.com/talks/elizabeth_loftus_the_fiction_of_memory.html

Marchant, R (2013) 'How young is too young? The evidence of children under five in the English criminal justice system' *Child Abuse Review* www.wileyonlinelibrary.com DOI: 10.1002/car.2273

McBride, A (2011) *Defending the Guilty: Truth and Lies in the Criminal Courtroom* (London: Penguin)

MoJ (2011a) *Achieving Best Evidence in Criminal Proceedings: Guidance on Interviewing Victims and Witnesses, and Guidance on Using Special Measures* (London: MoJ)

MoJ (2011b) *Family Justice Review: Final Report* (London: MoJ)

MoJ (2011c) *Family Justice Review: Interim Report* (London: MoJ)

MoJ (2012) *Registered Intermediary Procedural Guidance Manual* (London: MoJ)

MoJ (2013a) *Code of Practice for Victims of Crime* (London: MoJ)

MoJ (2013b) 'Victims to tell courts impact of crime' Press Release 29 October www.gov.uk/government/news/victims-to-tell-courts-impact-of-crime

MoJ (2013c) *Public Law Outline* (London: MoJ)

MoJ (2013d) *Witness Charter: Standards of Care for Witnesses in the Criminal Justice System* (London: MoJ) www.gov.uk/government/publications/the-witness-charter-standards-of-care-for-witnesses-in-the-criminal-justice-system

Munby, Justice (President of the Family Division) (2013a) 'View from the President's chambers (2): the process of reform – the revised PLO and the local authority' (London: MOJ) www.judiciary.gov.uk/wp-content/uploads/JCO/Documents/Reports/pfd-update-process-of-reform.pdf

Munby, Justice (President of the Family Division) (2013b) 'View from the President's chambers (3): the process of reform – expert evidence' (London: MOJ)

Munby, Justice (President of the Family Division) (2013c) 'View from the President's chambers (6): the process of reform – latest developments' (London: MOJ)

Munby, Justice (President of the Family Division) (2013d) 'View from the President's chambers (7): the process of reform – changing cultures' (London: MOJ)

Munby, Justice (President of the Family Division) (2013e) 'Transparency in the Family Courts and the Court of Protection: publication of judgments draft practice guidance' (MOJ: London)

Munro, E (2011) *The Munro Report of Child Protection: Final Report – A Child-Centred System* (London: DfE)

Murrie D, M Boccaccini, L Guarnera and K Rufino (2013) 'Are forensic experts biased by the side that retained them?' *Psychological Science* 24 October 1889–97

Norgrove, D (2011) *Family Justice Review Final Report* (London: MoJ, DfE and Welsh Government)

OPG (2007) *Making Decisions: The Independent Mental Capacity Advocate (IMCA) Service* (London: OPG) www.justice.gov.uk/downloads/protecting-the-vulnerable/mca/making-decisions-opg606-1207.pdf

Pitt-Payne, T (2013) 'Navigating the data maze' (book review: *Data Protection Law and Practice* (4th edition)) May *Counsel 39*

Plotnikoff, J and R Woolfson (2009) *Measuring Up? Evaluating Implementation of Government Commitments to Young Witnesses in Criminal Proceedings* (London: NSPCC/Nuffield Foundation)

Practice Direction 12A (2014) *Care, Supervision and Other Part 4 Proceedings: Guide to Case Management* www.familylaw.co.uk/system/uploads/attach-ments/0008/5147/PD12A_PLO.pdf

Practice Guidance (Transparency in the Family Courts) [2014a] EWHC B3 (Fam)

Practice Guidance (Transparency in the Court of Protection) [2014b] EWCOP B2

Rantzen, E (2013) 'Sharon Shoesmith: villain? Victim? Or someone who got it wrong?' 3 November *Daily Telegraph* www.telegraph.co.uk

Small, D I (2009) *Preparing Witnesses: A Practical Guide for Lawyers and their Clients* (Chicago/Washington: American Bar Association)
Spencer, J and R Flinn (1990) *The Evidence of Children: The Law and Psychology* (Oxford: OUP)
Spencer, J R and M E Lamb (2012) *Children and Cross-Examination: Time to Change the Rules?* (Oxford: Hart)
Swift, P, K Johnson, V Mason, N Shiyyab and S Porter (2013) *What Happens When People with Learning Disabilities Need Advice about the Law* (Bristol: Norah Fry Research Centre/University of Bristol)

Walport, M and R Thomas (2008) *Data Sharing Review Report* www.connecting-forhealth.nhs.uk/systemsandservices/infogov/links/datasharingreview.pdf
Wellman, F (1903) *The Art of Cross-examination* (London: Macmillan)
Wheatcroft, J M and L E Ellison (2012) 'Evidence in court: adult witness familiarisation and cross-examination, style effects on witness accuracy' 30 *Behavioural Sciences and the Law* 821–40
Wigin, C (2012) 'Child Q England's youngest witness' (July) *Counsel* 24–25

INDEX